inside the Jewelry Box

VOLUME 2

A Collector's Guide to

Costume Jewelry

Identification and Values

Ann Mitchell Pitman

COLLECTOR BOOKS

A Division of Schroeder Publishing Co., Inc.

Cover design by

Beth Summers

Book design by

Mary Ann Hudson

Cover photography by

Charles R. Lynch

COLLECTOR BOOKS
P.O. Box 3009
Paducah, Kentucky 42002-3009

www.collectorbooks.com

Copyright © 2007 Ann Mitchell Pitman

Searching for a Publisher?

We are always looking for people knowledgeable within their fields. If you feel that there is a real need for a book on your collectible subject and have a large comprehensive collection, contact Collector Books.

Proudly printed and bound in the
United States of America

Contents

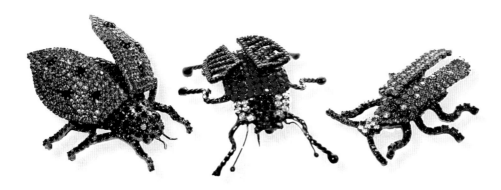

Acknowledgments

My beautiful daughter Ariel has once again brought a ray of sunshine to each and every day of my life, keeping me honest and making me think.

I have been blessed with many friends, and my little group has grown since my first book was published. Donna Burns, Laurie Mills, Carol Buckland, and Elizabeth Cooper are just a few of the friends I count on and are always just one phone call away with support or the right dose of humor. Kim Paff is always there to talk about jewelry, and whatever else needs to be discussed. Carol Buckland took the great photograph of me for this book. Eileen Holman likes me so much she sent me a pin that she knew I would love. Marianna Schweitzer outbid me for a fabulous magazine spread about Kenneth Jay Lane but she graciously made me color copies. My friends from Jewelcollect continually share with me and encourage me in my collecting and my research. I wish I had the space to list each and every name, but I will have to settle with remembering Laurel Ladd Ciotti, Cathy Gordon, Pat Seal, Bobye Syverson, Jane Clarke, Karen Bird, Karima Parry, Jan Young, and Erik Yang.

When my relatives first saw my book, they made me feel like a celebrity, so to Carmen, Tyler, and Austin Mitchell; John, Jake, and Sam Judy; Scott, Diane, Shane, and Kenya Pitman; Patrick Rogers; and Rockie, Nancy, Travis, and Ashlee Pitman, I thank you, for my 15 minutes of fame!

My first book was beautifully designed and published, and I would like to thank Billy Schroeder, Gail Ashburn, Amy Sullivan, Beth Summers, Mary Ann Hudson, and Kelly Dowdy. You all have once again turned my dreams into magic. Thank you.

My thanks go especially to Carol Bell, who loaned me her fabulous jewels to photograph for this book. Carol's booth, Treasures-In-Time, at the Carolyn Thompson Antique Mall at Hwy. 610 and Katy Road in Houston, Texas, is worth a trip from anywhere in the U.S to enjoy very high quality vintage costume jewelry. Carol even allowed me to photograph her own amazing personal collection. Thank you, Carol Bell.

To one of my favorite couples, Robert and Barbara B. Wood, thank you for everything, I love you both. Bobby Wood remains the greatest Texan I ever met in person. And Barbara, well, Barbara is totally amazing in every way, and you could not pray to the good Lord to bless you with a better friend.

Two jewelry designers loaned me lovely jewelry for the cover photograph for this book. These very talented jewelry designers make incredible handmade works of art. My sincere thanks go to Annie Navetta of Anni's Original Art Jewelry found at www.annisoriginalartjewelry.com and to Ian St. Gieler of Ian St. Gielar Costume Jewelry Design found at www.stanleyhaglernyc.com/home.htm. The lovely necklace I am wearing in my photograph was made especially for me by Annie Navetta.

Judy Miller, the Iris Lady, of Bangle Caddies and Vintage Costume Jewelry, found at www.banglecaddies.com, loaned me one of her wonderful bangle cradles to showcase my Bakelite bangles on the back cover. Thank you, Judy.

Special thanks go to Bettina and Michelle von Walhof for everything they did and their assistance with the chapter detailing their company. The pin I am wearing in my photograph is Madame Ant, a von Walhof creation.

Shortly before this book was completed, my doorbell rang and there was a special delivery from my dad, Charles John Mitchell, Sr. After half an hour of unwrapping, with shipping peanuts flying everywhere, I discovered a wonderful wooden box with different sizes of lined drawers, a mirror in the top and a plaque that duplicated the title of my book along with my name mounted on the very front. My dad saw it and thought it might be a good thing for me to use during book signings, to showcase some of my jewelry. He bought it and had it personalized with the plaque. I don't know that I can tell you what a treasure this is, and will always be to me. I love you, Dad.

And I can't forget my mom, Frances Eugenia Taylor Mitchell, who is the most beautiful person I have ever met. She is also smart and talented and pure joy to be around, in addition to having the most beautiful flower gardens in her neighborhood. I love you too, Mom.

The hardest thing to do is to tell my husband how glad I am to be married to him. We laugh our way through every day, and spend the last few minutes of each just talking. The good Lord blessed me when He brought you into my life. Each day's dance brings magic, I could accomplish nothing without you by my side. I dedicate this book to you, Tony, looks like we made it.

About the Author

In the days and months since my first book was published, I have met an astonishing number of collectors who have enriched my life. Many I correspond with via e-mail, and I have met a great many more during book signings. I have heard some incredible stories, like the one from the man who lived in Mexico as a child, near the Spradling workrooms. He said every visitor was marched down the street to the workrooms to purchase jewelry. Someone, somewhere, has the mate to the fabulous ruby red Mazer earring I wore to one signing at Borders and promptly lost. I hope they found something fun to do with it.

I continue to collect vintage costume jewelry, cruising the Internet every single day. I love it and it seems sometimes like that is the only thing I can talk about, but my husband remains amused and forgiving.

Since my first book came out I have only been able to add a very few pieces of signed Claudette jewelry to my jewelry box, but I think that is a good thing. It means collectors appreciate some of the things I have shared. What I have been able to add is some unsigned Claudette, which balances out my collection equation. I expect after this book comes out, it will be a long time before the clamor over California ceramic jewelry dies down enough for me to grab some more, but my collection is already enough fun, so I will be patient.

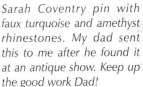

My collection grows almost daily, and I have been collecting now for 17 years. I wear most of what I collect, and have a few favorites. They are noted in the pages following. My greatest joy has been to see my daughter and my friends play in my jewelry box and come away with something they truly love. I had heard collecting friends in the past telling how they allowed friends and family to pick through their jewels and take some with them. I never understood until recently what joy you get when someone else's face lights up when you give them the very piece they are admiring. I vow to share more in the future, and I hope my daughter one day comes to love every single piece of jewelry inside my jewelry box.

I can be reached at annpitman@yahoo.com.

Sarah Coventry pin with faux turquoise and amethyst rhinestones. My dad sent this to me after he found it at an antique show. Keep up the good work Dad!

My husband was thrilled to spot this little pin in a box of mixed jewelry. The TCB stands for Taking Care of Business and was the motto of Elvis Presley, who passed out pins such as this one to his friends and family.

No description necessary for this girl who loves the slots. Welcome to Fabulous Las Vegas!

My dear friend Kim Paff brought this pin back for me from her trip to Paris.

New Orleans, Louisiana, bracelet in honor of one of my favorite cities.

Introduction

Welcome back to the wonderful world of vintage costume jewelry collecting. I hope you have fun as we continue our collecting journey. The book, again, is based on my column "Inside the Jewelry Box," which appears in selected antiques publications.

There have been a few changes since my first book. One has been finding and corresponding with collectors from all over the world. Each time I signed a book and shipped it to collectors around the United States, and then around the world, I marveled to think where each book was headed. I discovered that there were collectors so happy to find a treasure that they e-mailed a photograph as soon as they returned home. Many sent me photographs of examples of jewelry by Claudette and Calvaire that I had never before seen. An amazing few, including Eileen Holman and Elizabeth Cooper, even sent me gifts, which I proudly wear.

I was quite pleased to discover that, though there were mistakes in my first book, there were actually very few. My apologies to the Hobé family for calling their sons Robert and David when they are in truth Robert and Donald. And, the Les Bernard Jewelry Company was in business from 1963 until 1996. My sincere thanks to Lucille Tempesta of Vintage Fashion & Costume Jewelry (VFCJ) for her kind corrections. There, that wasn't so painful!

I have once again tried to give coverage to designers and companies who had been either overlooked or only briefly mentioned in other books. Some of the companies I have covered are not what is normally considered "vintage" but they are important companies making big contributions to the world of costume jewelry collectors, and they may very well be the highly sought after jewelry designers of the future. Their work speaks for itself and I hope you enjoy learning about these companies.

I would like to talk about pricing briefly. Most of the collectors I feature are also dealers and the jewelry I share is from their collections or their shops. The values given are from the price tags on most of this jewelry, so I consider them to be fair and current. As a collector only who cannot part with any of the jewels I buy, the pricing from my own collection comes from a combination of factors, including rarity and condition. If something is priced way out of range for the current market, it is probably because that item is dear to my heart and I could not be objective when pricing it. Or else I know something you don't know. Other than that, I stand by the values listed in this book.

There are a great many unsigned pieces of jewelry in this edition, I hope that if you see something you recognize, you will write to me with the designer information. Since many times a designer or manufacturer would only have one piece of jewelry from a set marked or signed, you may know the name of something in this book. The age-old question continues to plague me, as it does other collectors of vintage costume jewelry, why go to so much trouble to design such a thing of beauty and *not* put your name on it?

Many costume jewelry collectors are like myself, you may begin with only jewelry, but you eventually must branch out and add vanity accessories, compacts, gloves, handkerchiefs, handbags, perfume bottles, and hats. Oh, and scarves. And cigarette cases. Yes, I know that smoking is bad for you but these little beauties can be used for other things such as holding business cards or by adding a small mirror, as a completely different compact. Florenza recognized the need for all types of "girly" accessories, even making the most wonderful little bird saccharine holders, complete with tiny tongs. Look carefully on the front cover to spot my little gold saccharine bird, and my Napier jewelry holder girl vanity piece is on the back cover holding Lucite beads.

Grab a cup of coffee or tea or some Coca Cola and let's have some fun!

California Ceramic Jewelry

Flying Colors chili peppers necklace has nine chili peppers with black beads and gold-tone bead accents. The necklace is 21" long and the largest chili pepper is 2¼" long. **$150.00 – 195.00.** Author collection.

Lions, and tigers, and bears, oh my! The farmer in the dell. The Easter bunny. Alice in Wonderland. Noah's ark. Tropical rainforest with toucans and parrots and frogs. The circus is coming to town! Give the poor dog a bone. The cow jumped over the moon. How does your garden grow? Which came first, the chicken or the egg? Hard candy. Rich dark and creamy milk chocolates. Hear no evil, see no evil, speak no evil. All together, these may have little or no meaning, perhaps merely something to do with children's rhymes? Fairy tales? A youthful tea party?

In San Francisco, California, starting in 1975, these subjects and more came together to be represented in clay by a group of friends who were artists. A young woman by the name of Candace Loheed, whose interest in jewelry making started in college when she began making ceramic beads to complement some macrame jewelry, gravitated to San Francisco in the 1970s. There Loheed met Bean Finneran, the wife of her high school boyfriend. Finneran was doing ceramic sculptures and beads in her basement, which were very compelling. States Loheed, "a lump of clay and a day later I had made some very wonderful flowers as beads and she [Finneran] had made a lot of press molds which got converted into jewelry. We instantly knew we had something and decided to make jewelry into a business."

Loheed recalls the time with a pleasurable smile. "It was a very innocent time and we just forged ahead with very little idea of business. We called ourselves Parrot Pearls, which was a reflection of the color and whimsy of our work," she continues. "We took on two partners and set up a little studio in the attic of an old Victorian. It was a great time of creativity and there was a kind of magic happening ... even as we struggled to figure out how to do this," she remembers. "Sarah (Sally) Seiter, one of the new partners, had an interest in industrial design and her contributions helped get us into production. Bean Finneran had a unique sense of offbeat whimsy and we all shared a love of color and ceramics. I also enjoyed the business angle of things as well as the design and spent long hours happily absorbed in one or the other," Loheed states.

Color and whimsy are definitely the descriptive words used when viewing the work of the original Parrot Pearls Company. All of the jewelry has a very bold and bright look to it, even the pale pastels have a bright look. The ceramic beads used to complete each necklace are usually larger than those found on contemporary beaded necklaces. Most of the beads actually look like tasty pieces of candy, bright and shiny.

And the themes they chose have proven to be timeless. Collectors still fight over some of the jewelry when it comes to auction. All of the circus and farm themes are highly sought after, and bring high bids at auction. A recent necklace featuring all types of winged creatures, such as butterflies, dragonflies, and bees, sold for $244.00. A necklace of chocolates, some fairly oozing with cremes and fillings sold for $152.00. Alice and her friends in Wonderland sold for $177.50. A bright red chili peppers necklace sold for $108.42. A beaded necklace with a single camel bead sold for $57.67. A Little Jack Horner necklace sold for $101.00. Collectors still love the colorful whimsy that has continued with the appeal of the jewelry.

Loheed agrees. "The jewelry had an energy of its own, and buyers from all over got wind of this new jewelry and we enjoyed great success," she states. "We were busy growing and developing at a rapid rate. One partner dropped out and we moved to more industrial digs over in the China Basin district of San Francisco. We rented space of about 2,000 square feet and had hired a crew to help with production."

"We did shows all across the country, both commercial and American Craft council shows," Loheed continues. "It was a fun time. Our booth was

This amazing black, white, and yellow tropical fish necklace by Ruby Z is massive. The necklace is 22" long and the fish centerpiece is 3⅞" x 3⅛". These necklaces are actually very comfortable to wear. The necklace is signed on the blue bead at the clasp. **$150.00 – 175.00.** Author collection.

Here is an extremely rare Ruby Z necklace designed and signed by Bean Finneran. This necklace from the brush strokes line has a centerpiece measuring 3" in diameter, and the crazing was done at the time of the design. The necklace is 19½" long. The white bead at the clasp is signed "Ruby Z" on one side and "Bean Finneran" on the other. **$275.00 – 300.00.** Donna Burns collection.

always crowded and we wrote orders like mad, along with a sales rep we had hired to help us. The clay medium was fantastic and we could make anything and everything out of clay ... and we did!" she laughs.

There seems to be something for everybody in this category of California ceramic jewelry. Necklaces usually have a theme of one or multiple figures on a strand of vibrant beads. Alice in Wonderland has Alice, the Cheshire Cat, the Mad Hatter, and the White Rabbit. The pink elephants necklace has three elephants marching along. One necklace has imaginative dogs' heads. Another has a cat chasing a mouse. Penguins parade. Butterflies flutter. Guppies float. An aardvark ... sways. Clowns cavort. Cookies ... well, cookies just look edibly delicious.

Then there are the pins to tempt every collector too, many of which came in complementary pairs such as the doghouse and the dog bone, the mama bluebird flying down to feed the baby birds in the nest, the cow and the milk bottle, the crossword puzzle and the pencil, the dachshund and the hot dog wiener, a bunny and a carrot, and of course the chicken and the egg.

Bracelets proved to be a bit impractical so few were made, and buyers at the time wanted more necklaces than bracelets. The necklaces additionally came with hang tags, and the pins were on cards. The original retail prices for necklaces ranged from $30.00 to 300.00, and pins were priced from $12.00 to 30.00.

The process of designing the jewelry took many different forms, according to Loheed. "Some were drawn out in advance, a clay original would be made, and then a plaster mold for production purposes," she states. "Some, like the flowers, were made in clay by hand. We used a slab roller for some things and an extruder for the tubular beads. All the round beads were made meticulously by hand, mostly by subcontractors. We used some two part plaster molds of a commercial nature and made molds from almost everything that crossed our paths. We lived and breathed jewelry!" Loheed exclaims. "We had a huge spray booth to spray the glazes and many electric kilns for firing the beads. The pieces were all hand painted. Once an original was made, a crew of our artisans reproduced them from the original."

Loheed says, "We all had different styles and different work ethics and as women forging a business in the 1970s, we were kind of pioneers, feeling our way along. If you can imagine, there were no computers for business at that time!"

And as usually happens when someone has a good idea, trained employees eventually leave to start their own business making a different version of your product. People originally working for Parrot Pearls left and started their own company called Flying Colors. "They did quite well too, much to our annoyance, since they had felt free to use versions of our designs," Loheed remembers.

Other changes came about, and one of the original Parrot Pearls partners left. The remaining partners formed a new company they called Ruby Z. They moved into a new building and opened a fabulous studio of 8,000 square feet, with 14 employees, and many sales reps out selling the line to boutiques and department stores all over the country. Loheed continues, "We were ungodly busy and the demands of the business drove my last partner to leave the business. I continued on with the business for another 10 years. After my son was born, I drastically downsized and moved to wine country and had a tiny studio there amongst the grape vines in an attempt to 'chill out' and raise my son."

"Unfortunately, a very severe back operation forced me to put my business in storage and move back east to recover," she states. "And that is my story in a nutshell." According to Loheed, the original partners in Parrot Pearls were Bean Finneran, Sarah (Sally) Seiter, Nancy Fiddler, and Loheed. All of the partners have since gone their own ways, and are not in touch these days. Bean Finneran has remained in the San Francisco Bay Area and is a ceramic and installation artist, whose work is available at several Bay Area galleries.

Another oversize fish design from Ruby Z, this one is by Candace Loheed. The necklace in black and white is 19" long, with the fish being almost 5" long. The black bead at the clasp is signed "Ruby Z" on one side and "Candace Loheed" on the other. **$150.00 – 175.00.** Author collection.

Loheed still has some of the jewelry stock left and sells a piece every so often. "I have a few of the original designs and a few pieces of one-of-a-kind stock, and also some leftover production stock," she says. "I only go through it when I can, as I am busy with other things and want to move forward. Working with the old jewelry gives me mixed feelings. I have been amazed that there are still people avidly collecting the jewelry, even some who consider it vintage!" she laughs.

Loheed wants to move forward and has no interest in returning to the old style. "We started business in 1975 and I finally threw in the towel in 1995 ... so that was 20 years of ceramic jewelry," she states. "Needless to say, I lost count of how many designs we had, but it was hundreds and hundreds. Many were put into production and there were many one-of-a-kind and limited editions as well ... untold numbers of pins, earrings, necklaces, cords, etc."

Loheed now paints and is working on a new jewelry line. She lives near Chinatown in San Francisco and has a studio nearby. "I have been painting for several years, writing poetry, and now have been irresistibly drawn back onto making jewelry again," she says. "It is very different, as I have just turned 60 and have a different sort of life. You will recognize my style in the new jewelry, but it is very different at the same time." Loheed's current jewelry features crystals and beads from around the world, including semiprecious beads.

Almost all of the jewelry produced by these three companies was signed, if space allowed it to be signed. The necklaces are signed either on the back of the centerpiece, or on a bead at the clasp. Many of the Ruby Z necklaces have a round black or white bead that is painted with Ruby Z on one side and the artist name, such as Bean Finneran or Candace Loheed on the other side. The Parrot Pearls necklaces sometimes have the same black or white bead with the Parrot Pearls signature on it. Many of the necklaces are a single ceramic bead on a corded necklace, while others have coordinating beads all the way around beyond the centerpiece design.

This colorful dog pendant at first seems to be a Christmas design, with his big red bow tie, but the other colors like orange say he can be worn year round. Note the wonderful variety of bead sizes, shapes, and colors in the design. The necklace is 24" long, while the dog sits 3" tall. The necklace is signed on the white bead at the clasp with "Ruby Z" and "Candace Loheed." **$125.00 – 150.00.** Author collection.

The beads come in many sizes and styles, but one constant in the jewelry is the large size of it. Many of the centerpieces, such as the angel fish, are 3" or 4" tall. The centerpieces for each necklace vary from a single large "bead" to multiples such as the chili pepper with five peppers, the Christmas trees or the Christmas mittens with three each, or the carousel animals with seven. Odd numbers seem to hang better.

One of the best things about these necklace designs is that they are usually longer than standard necklaces, with many being 20" to 24", so they seem to fit today's collectors more easily. In addition, because of the standard screw-in clasp that most have, it is easy to find or make an extension of a couple of inches. They are also very comfortable to wear, though the larger designs can be a bit heavy. But you get used to it.

Each season brought design ideas to these companies. Christmas designs included trees, mittens, dogs, cats, light bulbs, and gift packages. Easter includes bunnies and eggs and carrots.

Halloween, of course, was witches and pumpkins. Valentines brought a plethora of heart designs, whether a single large heart or small matching hearts, or overlapping hearts, in candy colors or patterns. New Year's Eve saw a necklace filled with party noisemakers.

Springtime brought flowers of all types, and insects and butterflies, and seed packets and even a gardener's delight of radish, eggplant, corn, beet, carrot, squash, and cucumber. Summer saw sporting themes like bowling, and watermelons with seeds and boating flags and the circus and fish, oh the fish. You could have a big bold bright single fish or a passel of rainbow trout or even a school of guppies. How about the sailboat with a lighthouse and a flotation ring. Don't forget the beach balls.

Another black and white design, this one a smiling cat. This necklace is 18½" long and is signed on the black bead at the clasp with "Ruby Z" and "Candace Loheed." **$125.00 – 150.00.** Author collection.

The grapes theme has bunches of purple grapes interspersed with grape leaves on a chain of beautiful marbled green beads. The cherries necklace has cherries so realistic you might want to take a bite, with beads of black or white. And let's talk about breakfast. How about a black and white speckled chicken

between two vibrant fried eggs? Chickens were actually a popular design. Necklaces could feature a single chicken or a sweet white and black speckled chicken sitting on a nest surrounded by eggs and little chicks.

A family wearing polka dots and stripes. Tubes of paint in primary colors. Clowns dancing. Feathers fanned out. Noah's ark with the animals two by two. A bunch of bananas. Piggies off to market. And if nothing there intrigues you, then you should be able to find something in their abstract designs.

Even the names of the designs added to their whimsy and fun. Names such as Catch of the Day, Sharkbait, Long Suit, Guppies Galore, Scary Beast, Candies Deluxe, Puzzled Cats, and Holy Mackerel give some idea of the designers' imaginations.

Here is one of my favorite California ceramic necklaces, which is signed "Parrot Pearls" and has imaginative and extremely colorful animal head beads along with oversize and colorful beads. The white bead next to the clasp has "© Parrot Pearls" on it. The necklace is 20" long, the animal head beads are from 2" to 2¾" long. The fat little flat beads are an 1" in diameter. **$250.00 – 300.00.** Author collection.

In viewing all of the different designs, many collectors believe they can tell the difference between companies before turning the jewelry over to read the signature. Nearly all of the larger-than-life designs belonged to either Parrot Pearls or Ruby Z. Loheed agrees and believes this is due to the fact that they moved into the larger facility after a partner left and they moved into a new direction. "We had a new energy and wanted to go into new directions, as much as our customers would allow," she smiles. "Both myself and my remaining partner at the time have always been creative and when you have a good success, you get stuck in the rut of it ... it is harder to do new and innovative things. We were inspired by a new name and new space, and we just did different types of designs as we liked." She believes the owners of Flying Colors were more influenced by Parrot Pearls since that was the time and company where they trained and learned everything.

"We were flattered with copies, not only our employees who formed Flying Colors, but others as well. A French designer copied things in a milk-based plastic that were great, and included a vial of perfume in one bead on each necklace," she continues. "We got a wonderful package from India once with painted wooden copies. One of our former partners, Ms. Seiter, briefly had a company called Amazon Ice. I would say that other artisans and crafts people were also influenced by what we had done. We always had mixed feelings when we saw a new version of our designs, they say imitation is flattering!"

Loheed is pleased that today's collectors want her ceramic jewelry. "I think it is great that collectors bid enthusiastically (at online auctions) on the jewelry ... except for being called vintage ... I am not too keen on that!" she smiles.

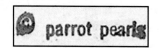

Parrot Pearls dog food bag pin. The pin is 3¼" and is stamped on the back. **$15.00 – 20.00.** Author collection.

Stamped signature on back of Parrot Pearls pin.

Parrot Pearls banana scatter pin is 2¼" and is stamped on the back. **$20.00 – 25.00.** Author collection.

Parrot Pearls penguin pin is 3¼" tall. It is stamped on the back. **$20.00 – 30.00.** Author collection.

Another of my favorite Flying Colors designs. This necklace has five little speckled hens marching along with red ceramic tube beads and two pairs of squat round black beads. The heart bead is marked "Flying Colors" on one side and "© 1981" on the other side. The necklace is 18" long and each hen is 1" tall. The farm designs are very popular with collectors. **$150.00 – 175.00.** Author collection.

Flying Colors watermelon and seeds necklace, pin, and earrings set. Here is the perfect set for a summer barbecue or a watermelon seed spitting contest at the Luling, Texas, Watermelon Thump Festival. Its very outrageousness makes is so appealing. The necklace is signed on the back of the slice and is 18" long, with the slice measuring 2½" x 1¼". The pin is 1⅞" and is stamped "Flying Colors." The earrings are 1½" and not marked but clearly part of the set. **$200.00 – 225.00.** Author collection.

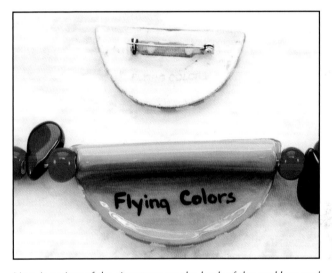

Here is a view of the signatures on the back of the necklace and the pin.

This Flying Colors cows necklace is 18¾" long. The center cow is signed on the back. **$100.00 – 125.00.** Author collection.

This Flying Colors necklace helps you get to sleep by counting sheep. The necklace has three jumping sheep with stars and pale blue beads. It is 18" long and each sheep is nearly 2" long. The center sheep is signed. **$150.00 – 175.00.** Author collection.

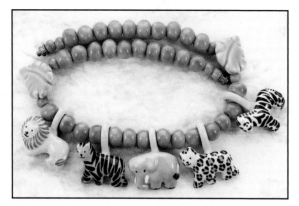

This Flying Colors jungle animals necklace is 18¾" long and the elephant is signed. **$125.00 – 150.00.** Author collection.

Tickle the ivories with this black and white piano keys necklace made by Flying Colors. The necklace is 17¼" long and is signed on the back of the first white bead key on the left. **$100.00 – 125.00.** Author collection.

Beads showing signatures of Candace Loheed, Ruby Z, and Bean Finneran.

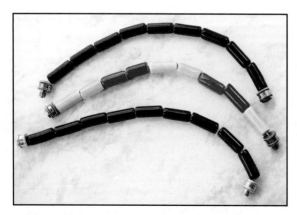

Sometimes the California ceramic necklaces are a little too short for today's collector, but these original extenders fix that little problem. And since they will be worn at the back of the neck, they are interchangeable with any of the necklace designs. Extenders range from 5½" to 6". **$20.00 – 25.00 each.** Author collection.

Flying Colors Christmas kitty in a fish box on the original card. Notice the tiny fish on the gift wrapping. The pin is signed on the back and is 1⅓" x 1½". **$20.00 – 30.00.**

A pair of Flying Colors scatter pins with the cow and the milk bottle. Pins range from 1¾" to 2" and both are stamped on the back. **$25.00 – 35.00.** Author collection.

A set of Flying Colors pins with mama blue-bird heading to the baby-filled nest. Both are signed. Mama is 2½" x 2¼" and babies are 1¹⁵⁄₁₆". **$25.00 – 35.00.** Author collection.

Who's in the dog house now? This Flying Colors set has the dog house and his little bone, only the house is signed. The house is 1¼" x 1⅛" and the bone is 1⅜". **$25.00 – 35.00.** Author collection.

This flying Colors green frog pin is signed and measures 2¼" x 1⅞". **$15.00 – 20.00.** Author collection.

This fabulous sunglasses scatter pin is signed "Flying Colors" and is 2½" wide. **$10.00 – 20.00.** Author collection.

I know nothing about the company that made this pin but believe it is from the same area and the same time frame as the previous California ceramic jewelry. The pin has an embedded stamp that reads " '82 HUEY" twice and an illegible mark alongside the copyright symbol. The pin is 2¼" long. **$10.00 – 15.00.** Author collection.

Back of pin showing embedded mark.

Alice Caviness

Alice Caviness sterling enameled bug pin with tiny red eyes, measures 1" x ¾". **$125.00 – 145.00.** Barbara Wood collection.

There is not very much information available on costume jewelry designer Alice Caviness. The manufacture of costume jewelry was a natural path taken by a woman who basically was a clothing designer. Her own factory produced her jewelry from the 1940s through the early 1960s. It was sold in exclusive boutiques on the East and West Coasts, and is by no means prolific. Many of the designs are breathtaking, large, and very bold. Caviness produced many designs of beaded necklaces.

Caviness is famous for her use of unusual combinations of colors and stones. Cherri Simonds in *Collectible Costume Jewelry* features a highly unusual set of rose jewelry. Alice had ivory carved and dyed a deep, bright, rose red for the flower heads, the leaves and stems were enameled green and brown with clear rhinestone accents. The styling is exquisite. Alice Caviness jewelry can be found marked "Sterling Germany" and also "1/20th 12kt. G. F." along with her name.

Alice Caviness died in 1983 but her company continued for a few more years before finally going out of business. Alice Caviness jewelry is uncommon, but well made and worth the price.

Here is a gorgeous Alice Caviness hinged clamper bracelet with pale orange cabochons and different colored rhinestones, accented with faux pearls. The bracelet is signed. **$350.00 – 395.00.** Carol Bell Treasures-In-Time collection.

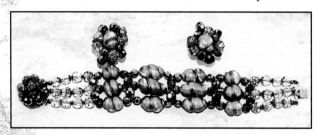

Alice Caviness bronze, crystal, and art glass set of bracelet with matching earrings. Notice the bronze beads hand wired onto the clasp. The bracelet is 7⅞" long and the earrings are 1⅛". Some of the art glass beads are suffering a slight loss of finish. **$175.00 – 200.00.** Author collection.

Alice Caviness black rhinestone cross pin/pendant and earrings features black cabochons. The pin is 3½" x 2½" and the earrings are ¾" x ⅝". Only the earrings are signed. **$195.00 – 225.00.** Carol Bell Treasures-In-Time collection.

This Alice Caviness set features crystal, gold chain, and baroque pearls in taupe and blue. The necklace is 16" long and the earrings are 1⅜" x 1". **$295.00 – 325.00.** Carol Bell Treasures-In-Time collection.

Alice Caviness parure with pin, bracelet, and earrings of ruby red and clear rhinestones. The bracelet is hinged. The pin is 2¾" and the earrings are 1" in diameter. **$250.00 – 325.00.** Carol Bell Treasures-In-Time collection.

Alice Caviness atomic style pin and earrings with blue olive cabochons. **$195.00 – 225.00.** Carol Bell Treasures-In-Time collection.

Lilly Daché

Lilly Daché was a fascinating woman. She was born in the town of Beigles, France, in 1898, though like most women of her time, she knocked five or six years off her age. Her career began at age 14 when she apprenticed to her aunt, who was a milliner, where she learned how to make hats. Reports vary about when she emigrated to the United States, basically because of the years she knocked off her age and her history, but she arrived in New York City in the early 1920s; after a short stay in Philadelphia where she worked and learned to speak English. Her book, *Talking Through My Hats,* published by Coward-McCann, Inc. in 1946, tells of her coming to New York in 1924 with $13.00 in her pocket.

Her second job was selling hats in Macy's Department Store but it only lasted six weeks. She left to return to work at the Bonnet Shop, her first job, which was located near the shops of Hattie Carnegie and Nettie Rosenstein. This was a time when women never left the house without wearing a hat and hats were the most important accessory, even more important than the dress. Most milliners of the time made hats for stock and had women sit in front of a mirror to try them on.

Daché was different from the beginning, mostly from necessity. When she and her girlfriend bought out the Bonnet Shop where they worked, there were no hats in stock for the first customer who walked in the door. Daché used her salesmanship to convince the customer to leave a small deposit and come back the next day for a hat designed just for her. Daché took the $2.00 deposit straight to the supply shops and bought what she needed to make the hat and returned to the shop to make it. The same thing was done with the next few customers until there were enough materials to begin making hats for stock. And a new way of making hats was born, where hats were designed and created to suit and flatter each individual customer, de-emphasizing one feature while emphasizing another.

Daché's hat business grew by leaps and bounds and she became *the* milliner to go to for hats. When her business got too big she moved to larger quarters, finally building her own nine story Lilly Daché building just off Park Avenue.

Daché is of course famous for her hats. She also wrote two books, in addition to the one mentioned previously, she wrote *Lilly Daché's Glamour Book* in 1956, published by J. B. Lippincott Company. This book explains how each woman can awaken feeling glamorous and retain the feeling throughout the day. This book is also quite amusing, with its outdated look at the way a woman dresses and takes care of herself, including what she terms "defuzzing" her legs.

Her book, *Talking Through My Hats,* is an autobiography, and makes for fascinating reading. She details her life and her work, and even describes her building, floor by floor. "The first floor is an entrance hall, behind thick glass doors, with a few showcases about, showing jeweled fripperies and perfume, mostly for atmosphere," begins the description. To the collector of vintage costume jewelry, this amounts to the most important piece of the puzzle of why Daché jewelry is so rare.

Many times throughout her books, she discusses her lines of hats, clothing, perfume, and cosmetics, but few mentions of the jewelry ever appear. One of the few times jewelry appears in her books is in the *Glamour Book* where she talks about how she herself dresses. "Most often during the daytime when I am busy you find me wearing a plain black dress with no trimmings, but maybe my one favorite jeweled pin and, of course, my many bracelets, without which I would not be caught dead, as you say," she tells us. Later on in the book she reveals that the average woman needs to wear a dramatic ring and lots of bracelets to draw attention to her hands and away from her less desirable features.

In a day and age when the word "rare" is so carelessly and incorrectly used, Daché jewelry is indeed rare. Most of the designs are what collectors would term "very nice." No attempts were made to copy famous or genuine jewelry. Jewelry was apparently only designed as a small sideline to accessorize the clothing and to add atmosphere to the showrooms. Few collectors have ever seen a piece of Lilly Daché's jewelry and few books have even mentioned her.

Both of Daché's books are captivating, showing what women of the time felt and how they lived. Collectors who specialize in 1940s and 1950s jewelry will especially appreciate this intimate look into those years. *Talking Through My Hats* is written as if the words came directly from the author's mouth, with no attempts to edit them, and they help bring her into view as a real person. Her words and phrases were cleaned up professionally for her *Lilly Daché's Glamour Book,* but her first book lets the reader come to know her intimately.

Her books tell her story nearly from birth, and relate many of the fascinating things that happened in her everyday life. She liberally drops names of the famous and the not-so-famous, including actresses and the social-ites of the time, even royalty. Many famous men brought their wives or girlfriends to see Daché, and they were of the movers and shakers of the times.

Daché relates the story of how one of her pansy hat designs was solemnly placed grave side after its owner somehow lost it at the church funeral service. Another time one of her hats solved the mystery of a suicide who checked into a hotel under an assumed name, without one piece of identification, but was traced through the number under the label of her Daché hat.

Daché tells how she made Gypsy Rose Lee angry, after refusing her second offer to strip at a charitable event, and how she planned an enormous party for all the "hot" designers, and what happened when she received a call from the secretary of Elsa Schiaparelli, who stated that "Madame was sorry but she would not be able to attend." Daché snapped "that was just fine, since Madame was *not* invited." She describes one of the lines of hats she designed with a veil of varying colors, with green over the eyes and pink over the cheeks, to give a woman's face color without her using makeup.

She tells how she designed a lovely pink room with padded walls in the Daché building for the ladies to use for a changing room but that she herself used when she felt the need to bang her head against the wall. Most interestingly, she tells how difficult it was to remain a woman of business but to drop everything and race home to glamorize herself for her husband's return from work. A woman of business during the day and the little wife in the evenings.

Daché led a very successful life, filled with love for her husband of 50 years, and was able to leave the life behind when they retired together to spend time in their homes in New York, Florida, Connecticut, and Paris. She left the business at a time when hats were beginning to fall out of popularity, and she herself stopped wearing them, and admitted to wearing wigs most of the time, since it made life simpler. She and her husband enjoyed 20 years of retirement together. Daché remained active in the world of fashion right up to her death on December 31, 1989 in a French nursing home. Her jewelry remains a great investment for collectors.

Lilly Daché clear rhine-stone pin with prong-set stones. The pin is 1¾" long. **$125.00 – 150.00.** Author collection.

Reverse view showing mark.

This gorgeous Lilly Daché clear rhinestone necklace is an amazing design which uses marquise, emerald, pear, round, and baguette rhinestones. The necklace is signed "Lilly DACHE" on the back of the flower-like pendant. Very rare. **$200.00 – 225.00.** Author collection.

Close-up view of the necklace centerpiece. Note: Please see my first book for a wonderful flower pin designed by Lilly Daché with red, green, and clear rhinestones.

Wendy Gell

Shades of purple highlight this gorgeous Wendy Gell necklace. **$175.00 – 200.00.** Carol Bell Treasures-In-Time collection.

The collectible costume jewelry field is a bit different from most antique and collecting categories. Contemporary costume jewelry can be as eagerly sought by collectors as vintage and antique jewelry. One example of this is jewelry by designer Wendy Gell, who continues her search for one of the Jessica Rabbit pins she created for the movie *Roger Rabbit*.

How could a designer end up searching for one of her own designs? You would think she would have multiple examples of everything she designed in her own collection. But that's not always the way it works, according to Gell. "The pins were so popular they sold completely out of the limited quantities before I could get my hands on one." Her relationship with Disney lasted for five years, and her "totally pavéd" jewelry from that period during the mid-eighties has collectors scrambling to add one to their own collections.

Wendy Gell has been designing jewelry for 30 years. She has always been an artist, first and foremost, and turned to jewelry when her career as a songwriter ended after she and her partner went their separate ways. Gell tried lots of things at that time, including driving a taxi in New York. She returned to her artist background and tried her hand at a variety of different mediums before she "hit on jewelry."

Gell is the original rags to riches story, beginning with a few pieces of jewelry she designed and put together at her dining room table, and sold in a few boutiques in New York. She experienced slow steady growth as her work found collectors, including Liberace, Elton John, Cher, and Elizabeth Taylor, and then she was discovered by Disney. "Working with Disney was totally like a dream, so glamorous, meeting Steven Spielberg, being invited to great parties… it was the most fun I've ever had," she says. "I take more pride in my work with Disney than I do anything else."

Fellow jewelry designer Brenda Sue Lansdown believes that Wendy Gell is the Andy Warhol of her media. "Wendy's jewelry is heart jewelry. Her handmade pieces come from inside her. I have loved her bright spirit, her joy, and her whimsical nature for years," Landsdown states.

A look at the current offerings on her website (wendygell.com) might cause you to grab the telephone and your checkbook. Her jewelry has everything collectors are seeking: rhinestones, great designs, and classic, bold, or humorous offerings in standard necklaces, bracelets, earrings, and brooches, and more unusual barrettes. Her site is a pleasure to "stroll" around. The Gold Chain bracelet she offers in her "wristies" collection is described as "Very easy to wear. Very hard to make." Her Isis bracelet states it is "a museum piece for the stones alone." Her Turquoise 2 wristie is "a huge chunk of amber, has bugs and rainbow." Bonzer Dog Bones pins are pink or lime green plastic bones inset with rhinestones. Her Pink Mushies are pink rhinestone encrusted mushrooms, and her adorable Ahoy, Maties! pin features a pair of sailors who are "chipper in their blue and white enamel suits with crystal shirts and pearl heads." Prices range from $3,000.00 for the Isis bracelet to $40.00 for Ahoy, Maties!

You may wonder why this month's column features a contemporary designer. First of all, I did promise from the beginning that we would cover contemporary jewelry. Second, and most important to me, is the fact that vintage costume jewelry collectors rarely have the opportunity to collect first hand the pieces future collectors will be seeking. Our mothers and grandmothers were around for Coco Chanel, Hattie Carnegie, and Miriam Haskell. Maybe Wendy Gell is "our" designer.

Note: Wendy has added a great many different things to her website, since this column originally ran, in addition to her jewelry. Prices start around $35.00 for her handmade hair barrettes, and go up for pins and wristies. Make sure to check out Wendy's oil paintings.

I call this Wendy Gell wristie the Bathing Beauty. A lovely lady in a bathing cap and shoes and wearing an ankle bracelet reclines on a flowered jewel beside a butterfly and a gazing ball. Like most Wendy Gell wristies the cuff bracelet is covered with rhinestones. It is signed and dated 1986. The bracelet is 3½" wide. **$2,000.00+.** Barbara Wood collection.

This Wendy Gell wristie has red flowers set around an Eisenberg Original pin. This is a large wristie, 4" x 5", and it is signed and dated 1986. **$950.00 – 1,050.00.** Barbara Wood collection.

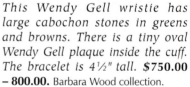

Wendy Gell signature plaque.

This Wendy Gell wristie has large cabochon stones in greens and browns. There is a tiny oval Wendy Gell plaque inside the cuff. The bracelet is 4½" tall. **$750.00 – 800.00.** Barbara Wood collection.

This lovely flower garden wristie features pink leather flowers and small porcelain flowers. This wristie is signed and dated 1986 and is 3½" wide. **$500.00 – 550.00.** Barbara Wood collection.

This wristie has a large lavender center stone and looks like a winter scene. It is 4" tall and has the signature plaque inside. **$1,000.00 – 1,100.00.** Barbara Wood collection.

I call this wristie the Maharani because it looks like a fancy crown. It is almost 5" tall. The bracelet is signed and dated 1986. **$850.00 – 950.00.** Barbara Wood collection.

This wristie is designed around a golden slice of a nautilus shell. It has a different design from most Wendy Gell wristies. It is 3½" tall and is signed and dated 1987. **$700.00 – 775.00.** Barbara Wood collection.

Wendy Gell Nautilus wristie with two sliced nautilus and rock crystals. The bracelet is over 3" tall and over 1" high on the cuff. The bracelet is signed and dated 1987. **$750.00 – 825.00.** Barbara Wood collection.

This Wendy Gell bangle bracelet has brown and orange stones. It is 1½" wide and is signed and dated 1982. **$195.00 – 225.00.** Barbara Wood collection.

Here is a Christmas themed Wendy Gell bracelet with Santa heading off to make his deliveries. A tame design compared to most Wendy Gell wristies. **$125.00 – 150.00.** Carol Bell Treasures-In-Time collection.

Wendy Gell collage pin looks like a comet with a trailing tail, or a flower with a large leaf. The pin is nearly 4" long. **$95.00 – 115.00.** Barbara Wood collection.

Wendy Gell Mickey Mouse rhine-stone and faux pearl pin, 3½" x 3¼". **$1,500.00+.** Barbara Wood collection.

Here is the smaller version of the Wendy Gell Mickey Mouse, note the difference of the seed pearls on the eyes. This pin is 2" long. **$150.00 – 175.00.** Barbara Wood collection.

I believe this Mickey Mouse golfer is a Wendy Gell for Disney design. He is 2" tall. **$65.00 – 95.00.** Barbara Wood collection.

I think this is also a Wendy Gell for Disney Mickey Mouse pin. He is 2½" tall and is signed Disney. **$225.00 – 250.00.** Barbara Wood collection.

Wendy Gell Disney Donald Duck pin with rhine-stones and faux pearls. The pin is 2" tall. **$150.00 – 165.00.** Barbara Wood collection.

Wendy Gell Disney Daisy Duck pin, 2½" tall. **$95.00 – 105.00.** Barbara Wood collection.

Wendy Gell Andy Warhol-inspired kissable mouth pin from Diamonds Are a Girls Best Friend *starring Marilyn Monroe, 3½" x 2".* **$850.00 – 950.00.** Barbara Wood collection.

Wendy Gell collage earrings from the 1970s feature hematite-type stones with a variety of other colored stones. All the stones are glass. One earring has the Wendy Gell signature plaque. The earrings are 1⅞" x 1¼". **$90.00 – 115.00.** Barbara Wood collection.

Ann Vien

These Ann Vien earrings have a large blue art glass cabochon accented with sky blue rhinestones. The earrings are 1½" x 1". **$65.00 – 75.00.** Author collection.

A few years ago when looking through some of my jewelry reference books, I ran across the name Ann-Vien. Many times when I see the name of a jewelry designer or company that is rarely mentioned, I start looking for those pieces to add to my own collection. I have been pretty successful with collecting Ann Vien.

There are two marks for Ann Vien jewelry, one is "ANN VIEN" and the other is "ANN-VIEN," the only difference being the added hyphen. The matching pieces are easily identified once you have the earrings, as you will see from the following examples of Ann Vien jewelry.

I have not been so successful when researching Ann Vien. The only things I know about this company/designer is that it/she was located in Atlanta, Georgia, around 1950. Many of the pieces of jewelry I have found are beaded, though I have seen a few rhinestones pieces. I will continue to research this designer/company and hope to bring you more information in my next book.

In the meantime, please enjoy these pieces from my collection. The earrings are marked, but not the necklaces, though there is plenty of space on the necklaces to place a signature plaque. I have seen a couple of bracelets with a metal hang tag, but signed bracelets are rare. Knowing the signed earrings is the key to finding the matching pieces.

A truly rare find, this AB (aurora borealis) rhinestone set has large links set with AB stones with an open back setting. The necklace is very heavy. It measures 17½" and each link is ¾" in diameter. The earrings are both marked and the AB rhinestones in them are prong set, unlike the necklace. The earrings are 1" in diameter. **$400.00 – 450.00.** Author collection.

Reverse view of earring showing mark.

Pink art glass with lavender and black glass beads and faux pearl beads make up this Ann Vien set. The necklace is 58" long and has no marks on it. The earrings, both of which are marked, are 1⅜" dangles. **$200.00 – 250.00.** Author collection.

Red and black glass bead necklace and earrings. Notice the black beads are the same as the ones in the previous set. This three-strand necklace is 13" long with a 3" extension. The earrings are both marked and are 1½" x 1¼" with dangle beads and a design that shows the filigree mounting. **$195.00 – 225.00.** Author collection.

This set with gold-tone beads looks brand new and never worn. The five-strand necklace is actually lightweight and is 13" long with a 3" extension. The earrings are both marked and dangle 1¾". **$150.00 – 175.00.** Author collection.

Gorgeous green art glass cabochons are accented with shapes and shades of green rhinestones in this Ann Vien pair of earrings. Both are signed and they measure 1⅜" x 1¼". I believe once collectors see these earrings and those on the top left of page 22, they will find the rest of the set in their own collections attributed to another designer. **$65.00 – 75.00.** Author collection.

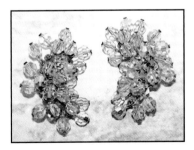

Another quite beautiful pair with the same finding as the orange and amber earrings to the right. These earrings have jonquil AB crystal beads. Both are signed and are 2¼" x 1¾". **$55.00 – 75.00.** Author collection.

Another completely different look from Ann Vien with a beautiful faux pearl centerpiece and rhinestone dangles. Note the rhinestone dangles are attached between the beads. The necklace is 12" long with a 2½" extension and the earrings are 2¾" x 1½". The large faux pearl stones are glass and both earrings are marked. **$165.00 – 195.00.** Author collection.

Tiny black AB beads make up this pair of Ann Vien dangle earrings, which are 1¼" long. **$25.00 – 45.00.** Author collection.

Pale gray faux pearl dangles and rhinestone rondelles make up this pair of Ann Vien earrings, both of which are signed. The earrings dangle 1½". This pair has a Haskell look to them. **$45.00 – 55.00.** Author collection.

Completely plain pair of Ann Vien earrings in silver tone with a swirled leaf motif. Both are signed and are 1¼" long. **$15.00 – 25.00.** Author collection.

 I have seen quite a few Ann Vien earrings with this particular finding. These have an unusual color combination with the orange and amber and then one big blue bead. The design of the earrings goes up the ear. They are both signed and are 2" x 1¾". **$25.00 – 45.00.** Author collection.

These earrings are stunning in their simplicity. They have an AB finish inside the oversized cabochon and are beautifully mounted. The cabochons look dark pink-ish until they pick up all of the surrounding lights. Both are signed and they are 1" x ¾". **$65.00 – 75.00.** Author collection.

Reverse view showing signature.

Elzac

Perky little Elzac lady with red leather hat and collar. **$125.00 – 150.00.** Kim Paff collection; photo courtesy of Kim Paff.

Elzac is a funny word to say. Elzac jewelry is fun to look at. And Elzac jewelry is fun to collect, too. Nearly every collector I run into has at least one Elzac pin in their collection. Most of the pins feature a ceramic face or body, and is outlined or accented with Lucite. There are all types of animals, from the jungle to the backyard, and of course there are the Victims of Fashion pins.

These Victims of Fashion pins usually feature the face of a woman, though there are some with men, and a rare few have a full body; most are merely the neck and head. All types of materials were used to accent the faces, including yarn, feathers, cloth, and fur, among other things. The bad thing about Elzac pins is that they are not signed, so collectors are making educated guesses about what is and isn't a true Elzac.

The Vintage Fashion and Costume Jewelry (VFCJ) newsletter carried a story by author Kathy Flood about Elzac jewelry in its Volume 14 Issue #2, which detailed how to identify Elzac and showed a variety of pins. The Italian Brunialti book *A Tribute to America* shows these pins with patents and ads. Author Kathy Flood discovered that Elliot Handler, the man who designed these pins, was also the man who later started Mattel. The pin with blond pigtail braids was named Daisy, while the lady with Coralene (sugared look beads) fruit and flowers on her hat was called South American Belle. She wears a very haughty look, and it is one collectors can't seem to resist.

Elizabeth Cooper of Chattanooga, Tennessee, is a dealer who stumbled upon an Elzac Victim of Fashion lady. "I snapped her up right away because she seemed to demand that I take her home with me. She has set on my desk for weeks now, and she has decided to stay," says Cooper. "I just can't give her up!" she laments.

Lisa Corcoran of Jazzle Dazzle found at www.jazbot.com/Shop agrees with Cooper. "I am attracted to the whimsical and out-of-the-ordinary," Corcoran says, "and the Elzac Victim of Fashion pins make me smile. They are totally unpretentious and don't take themselves too seriously. Dare to wear one of these and you will always get noticed!" she states.

"Elzac made creative use of materials, such as Lucite, felt, leather, yarn, and fur, not to mention elaborate headdresses, and produced such a variety of faces and ethnicities that I am always delighted to come across ones I have never seen." Corcoran continues, "Some of these faces have serious attitude. I think the gussied-up saloon dames have to be my favorite ... but wait! ... there is the cheeky monkey! ... and oh the Eskimo babies in their furry hoods. How about the Betty Grable? And oh wait!" she laughs. Dealer Laurel Ladd Ciotti of Eclectica Vintage Jewelry and Collectibles, found at eclecticala.com has sold a great many of these beauties over the years, and now regrets seeing them leave her possession. "I think they are ingenious and I love that each one was unique," she states. "I wish I had back in my possession, each and every one I ever sold so I could put them in a shadow box and enjoy them as folk art."

Cathy Gordon is a preeminent collector who speaks highly of this jewelry. She starts by saying, "You can't own just one. My first Elzac, and I definitely didn't know it was an 'Elzac,' was a Josephine Baker type purchased for my blackamoor pin collection. But these pins have radar — once they know there is a welcoming home, they find you. Before long, three more had joined Josephine. I found it fascinating," she continues, "to see what could be done with the same basic face mold by changing the skin color and adding different hats and doodads. A female could easily become a male! I hit the jackpot at an antique show, one seller had a dozen of the lovely ladies, all with hats and feathers. I told her I had a boarding house, so home they came with me."

"I was told these were called Victims of Fashion, never did find out why," Gordon continues. "I was fascinated enough that I started looking for them. I found a few on some websites and discovered there were animals! What fun! The faces, styles, and colors were ever changing, but common characteristics were the ceramic forms, usually with a curly Lucite appendage, such as the tail on a monkey or the stick of a hobby horse. Sometimes there was real animal fur, looking like a bad toupee!" Gordon laughs.

Elzac blue squirrel pin is called Shy Squirrel and is 2½" tall. **$100.00 – 125.00.** Barbara Wood collection.

Gordon has apparently put a lot of time into searching for and researching this jewelry. "The most uncommon Elzac pins are full figured. I have found a ballerina and a Chinese water carrier. There are some Lucite/wood combinations attributed to Elzac, but these were a common design from the same time period, so they are more difficult to confidently ascribe to any particular company," she says.

"In general," Gordon continues, "the construction on Elzac jewelry is unremarkable, but this is not surprising as these were made during WWII when metal was generally unavailable. The humans are made using a standardized group of head shapes, most of which were patented, with the faces in different skin tones. I suspect some of my more individualistic pieces were earlier models, made before Elzac transitioned the lines to a few heads."

"There are a lot of animals — like the humans, the ceramic bodies come in a variety of colors and with different tails and decorations. The pin backs are very cheap and simple. Some have been molded into the ceramic while others are glued to the backs, perhaps because the pin came off at some time," she speculates. "There is a series of 'twins' whose heads are connected by a wooden backing piece. None of my pins are signed, though Elzac made ceramic animals which had paper tags. I do not believe Elzac made anything but pins for its jewelry line," Gordon concludes.

Elzac jewelry was made starting around 1941 and is fun for any collector. Keep your eyes peeled when peering into those showcases and you just might find someone staring back at you.

Elzac green monkey pin with Lucite tail and a leather and wood button cap. He is 2½". **$100.00 – 125.00.** Barbara Wood collection.

Elzac green horse pin with yellow Lucite mane and tail is 1¾" x 3". **$100.00 – 125.00.** Barbara Wood collection.

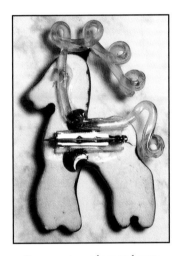

Reverse view of green horse.

Elzac yellow carousel horse with Lucite pole is 2¾" x 4". **$100.00 – 125.00.** Barbara Wood collection.

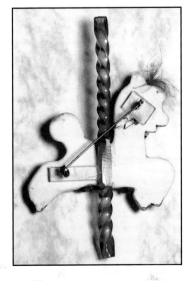

Reverse view of carousel horse.

Elzac lady in green with red Lucite head piece. **$150.00 – 200.00.** Kim Paff collection; photo courtesy of Kim Paff.

This stylish Elzac lady has a tiny little pouf of hair. **$100.00 – 150.00.** Kim Paff collection; photo courtesy of Kim Paff.

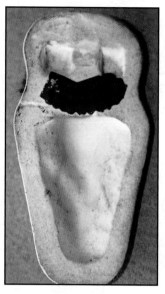

Reverse view of lady with her tag still on.

This aloof Elzac lady wears a cutting edge Lucite hat. **$125.00 – 150.00.** Kim Paff collection; photo courtesy of Kim Paff.

High-fashion Elzac dame with red pompon hat. **$100.00 – 125.00.** Kim Paff collection; photo courtesy of Kim Paff.

Elzac Victim of Fashion with yellow Lucite. **$100.00 – 125.00.** Kim Paff collection; photo courtesy of Kim Paff.

Juliana

Much has been learned about Juliana jewelry since my first book. For one thing, collectors now call it Delizza & Elster Juliana. My friend Jan Young is the moderator of the online D&E Juliana group on Yahoo and I asked her to tell collectors more about the jewelry and joining the group.

Interest in vintage costume jewelry is on the rise again and is attracting the attention of a new generation of collectors. If you collect what catches your eye, it is entirely possible that a portion of your vintage jewelry is unsigned. Wouldn't it be exciting to learn how to determine if the jewelry you own was an unsigned Juliana or a piece manufactured by DeLizza & Elster (D&E)? If you are interested in learning from people who specialize in collecting this type of jewelry and who continue to play an important role in the research of such, you should consider joining the Discovering Juliana/D&E Jewelry group on Yahoo.

DeLizza & Elster (D&E) manufactured jewelry for more than 50 years and for hundreds of companies during that time period. There was also a Juliana Original company that made jewelry for approximately two years in the 1960s, marked with a hang tag. The former president of both companies is our mentor and provides us with valuable insight into how the jewelry was created, manufacturing tidbits, and answers to our questions.

Thanks to our members, we have the largest collection of D&E and Juliana-attributed jewelry found in one single database. Our collection of photos includes a known attribute section, triage center, voting and poll results, training section, verification request center, jewelry made for other companies section, and many more.

Being specialized allows us the time to focus and become proficient in the history and attributes of D&E and Juliana jewelry. We host a variety of different events online to make your learning and collecting experience enjoyable. Membership is restricted, active participation is completely voluntary.

To view our main page or to join, go to groups.yahoo.com/group/discoveringjulianajewelry. To view a sampling of our database of photos, go to imageevent.com/discoveringdandejewelry.

Every time I get a new DeLizza & Elster Juliana bracelet, I tell myself, "Oh, THIS one is my favorite." But I love them all. This one is particularly beautiful as it has my favorite pastel shades of crystal beads and each link is also set with large prong set rhinestones. It has the matching pin and earrings. The bracelet is 7" long with the five links. The pin is 2¾" and the earrings are over 1". **$450.00 – 550.00.** Author collection.

This gorgeous pink bracelet is a Delizza & Elster Juliana design. All the rhinestones are prong set and the marquise stones have an open back. The bracelet is 7¼". **$125.00 – 150.00.** Author collection.

This fun bracelet is another of the Delizza & Elster Juliana line. I don't know what these lightweight white beads are called but I call them popcorn beads. There are three attached to each link. Each link also has small pink stones and clear and pink givré stones. The bracelet is 7¼". **$125.00 – 150.00.** Author collection.

Juliana speckled art glass bracelet with green prong set rhinestones. Like all of the jewelry in this line, this bracelet came in a wondrous variety of colors. My first book has this same bracelet in green and black stones. The bracelet is 7½". **$175.00 – 195.00.** Author collection.

Pink marquise and AB stones Juliana pin with matching earrings. Marquise stones are unfoiled and open backed. The pin is 2" in diameter and the earrings are 1¼" long. The matching bracelet is shown in my first book. **$95.00 – 125.00.** Author collection.

Unsigned D&E Juliana two-tone blue pin with matching earrings. The marquise stones are in three different shades of blue, and every other stone is set open back. The pin is 2¾" x 1" and the earrings are 1½" long. **$95.00 – 120.00.** Carol Bell Treasures-In-Time collection.

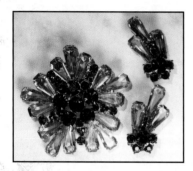

Gorgeous unsigned Juliana blue rhinestone pin with matching earrings. The pin is 3½" x 1½" and the earrings are 1½" x ⅞". **$120.00 – 145.00.** Carol Bell Treasures-In-Time collection.

Reverse view of pin.

Fun unsigned Juliana pin with dangling blue art glass beads, measures 3" x 1½". **$115.00 – 125.00.** Carol Bell Treasures-In-Time collection.

Reverse view of pin.

Beautiful unsigned Juliana pin with dangling art glass beads, 3½" x 1½". **$115.00 – 125.00.** Carol Bell Treasures-In-Time collection.

DeRosa

DeRosa jewelry has what I call the "ooh-ahh factor," you see a piece of it and you say "ooh" then you turn it over to see the DeRosa signature and you say "ahh." DeRosa was a family business started by Ralph DeRosa in the early 1930s and run by his family until around 1970. The business was based in New York City.

DeRosa jewelry is a bit difficult to find. Because of its beauty and quality, most owners hold onto the jewelry. Even if they don't wear costume, they can still appreciate the exceptional designs of DeRosa. Most DeRosa jewelry features classic and timeless designs, such as the line of floral beauties. Every decade has its floral inspired jewelry; even a walk through the jewelry offerings at a department store today will reveal plenty of flower pins. That means collectors will keep this jewelry to wear again and again, year after year.

DeRosa jewelry features many designs in addition to florals. Their figurals include birds, fish, dogs, insects, and even fruit, among others. Pearls were quite prominently used, as well as large and beautifully made colored rhinestones.

Ralph DeRosa was among the costume jewelry manufacturers whose jewelry mimicked the real thing. Much of their jewelry was mounted in sterling vermeil. The enameling on DeRosa pieces appears to have been done by extremely talented artists, and not just whoever happened to be assigned to enameling on that particular day in the manufacturing plant.

Signed DeRosa pieces are hard to find because many pieces left the manufacturer with paper tags. This makes a reference such as hand-painted illustrations invaluable. One place to view some incredible artwork along with some of the jewelry it portrays is the website of Jane Clarke, dealer and collector extraordinaire. Her website, found at www.morninggloryantiques.com, has a great many reference pages and details DeRosa through jewelry and these illustrations she was fortunate enough to acquire. Says Clarke, "In my opinion, DeRosa jewelry is the apex of costume jewelry design, detail, and dimension. Most pieces from the 1940s are extremely substantial and well made, three-dimensional, and they utilize a combination of sterling vermeil, rhinestones and/or artificial pearls, and enameling. The original artwork and finished pieces show a fascinating progression from the designer's mind to the end product, sometimes with hand-written notes as to changes and finishing details." Clarke concludes, "DeRosa is this long-time collector's jewelry of choice!"

Cheri Van Hoover of Milky Way Jewels, found at www.milkywayjewels.com, agrees with Clarke. "I love the classic lines and elegance of DeRosa pieces. DeRosa designs have a richness and sophistication rarely matched by other designers," she says. "The beauty of the enameling on DeRosa is unsurpassed. Combined with the elegance and grace is a playful quality, a sort of joie de vivre, that always lifts my spirits to see or wear," Hoover states.

The timeless beauty of DeRosa jewelry makes all collectors dream of adding a piece or two to their own collections. Everything about the design, from exquisite stones to artistic enameling to the breathe of inspiration each piece seems to exude, especially the jewelry made during the 1940s, speak well for the continuing value of this company's jewelry. The next time you see a magnificent sparkler in a showcase and say "ooh," you might shortly be saying "ahh, DeRosa."

This stunning fur clip is signed "Sterling RDEROSA" and was made by Ralph DeRosa. It has a beautiful sapphire blue stone and clear accents around the design. 3⅝" tall. $275.00 – 325.00. Author collection.

Reverse view showing signature.

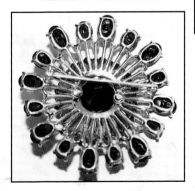

DeRosa sterling gold washed pin with red cabochons and a navy blue cabochon center. The pin is signed "R DeRosa" and "Sterling" and measures 2½" in diameter. $295.00 – 325.00. Carol Bell Treasures-In-Time collection.

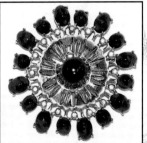

Reverse view of pin.

Bettina von Walhof

This Bettina von Walhof seahorse pin is nearly 5" tall with an amber rhinestone body and a little green eye. **$300.00 – 325.00.** Barbara Wood collection.

Most collectors of vintage costume jewelry prefer rhinestones, are especially fond of figurals, and are crazy for anything over-the-top. Bettina von Walhof designs fit that bill in all three categories.

Bettina von Walhof is a bit different from most jewelry designers. On her fiftieth birthday, she decided to do something she had always wanted to do, that was simply to create. Von Walhof was a long time collector of vintage costume jewelry, with a concentration of 1940s and 1950s jewelry. Like many collectors, she also loved the big bold pieces but couldn't find designs that suited her particular likes, one of which was insects.

Von Walhof is a nature lover, and she decided to create some pieces of jewelry that appealed to her, and defined her own personality. She had friends in the costume jewelry industry, like Larry Vrba, David Mandel, and Robert Sorrell who encouraged her in her endeavors. People who already have a strong presence in your selected field are the best friends you could have, as their encouragement and suggestions will help you succeed.

And succeed von Walhof did, says Michelle von Walhof, Bettina's daughter. "Her first jewelry creations, though primitive in design, were full of character, packed with style, and they became an instant success," says Michelle. "Her designs were so fresh and innovative she was asked by Kenneth Jay Lane to come and work for his company," reveals Michelle. But Bettina chose not to work for him.

Instead, Bettina von Walhof contemporary jewelry designer was born. Bettina labored over every aspect of her jewelry designs alone. "Each piece is handmade, using only the best Swarovski crystals," states Michelle. "It can take up to four weeks from start to finish for one small piece, up to one year for the very large exclusive pieces. Each stone is prong set by hand and must then be soldered and finally plated giving it the von Walhof's signature dark hematite color," says Michelle.

"Only signature Swarovski crystals are used unless a piece is being made with vintage stones. Necklaces and earrings are made with rare vintage molded glass, plastic, hand-painted beads, antique china, and semiprecious stones," she continues. "Because they do not limit themselves to one genre or medium, the designs can range from the serious to the silly. The only limitation is imagination," states Michelle.

From the beginning, Bettina's jewelry designs were a huge hit with collectors. Some of von Walhof's customers include Madeleine Albright, Art Buchwald, and Ineke Hauer. Her most famous client is the "grand dame of glitz Liza Minelli," Michelle admits proudly. Bettina's trademark became the word "large" and her motto is "Jewelry for Confident Women."

Bettina von Walhof designs are amazing. Almost all of the vintage creations are oversized when compared to most rhinestone jewelry. Many of her designs, such as those figurals with heads, are also tremblers. Her red lobster is designed so that all of his claws and tentacles move as you move. The squid pin from the Sea Beasties line has eight legs that tremble and move. The skeleton pin is hinged so his entire body shakes, rattles, and rolls. The Area 51 alien has trembling arms and legs, as do the robots. The egrets wing flaps and the rockin' retro Santa has swivel hips, just like Elvis.

In 2004, the company took a slight turn. Bettina's daughter Michelle, who had been working for her mother for years behind the scenes, sat down in front of the workbench and started playing with the findings and rhinestones. Like her mother, Michelle loved vintage jewelry and most especially the 1940s and 1950s jewels. Her intrigue with the world of jewelry design and creation caused her to use those findings and rhinestones to create a poodle pin for herself to wear to a party. She was nervous about what Bettina might say when she saw that Michelle had been in her work space, but she need not have worried. Bettina was so pleased with the poodle that she was immediately named Miss Priss The Pink Poodle and Michelle and her designs joined Bettina's, and the name of the company was changed to von Walhof Creations.

Red-wing bug with trembler wings, 2½" long. **$125.00 – 150.00.** Barbara Wood collection.

Their jewelry is signed B+M von Walhof. They still make large jewelry, but they also make smaller designs, making their jewelry affordable to every collector. This is a big plus when you consider that the von Walhof red lobster that is almost 8" long sells for nearly $1,300.00. You can find the von Walhof jewelry at www.rubylane. com/shops/thecuriosityshop2 starting as low as $20.00. The larger designs are also available, and most are limited editions of one, eight, ten, or twelve. A cruise through their web pages will reveal cats, dogs, flowers, shrimp, foxes, ferrets, mice, birds, bunnies, cows, chameleons, holiday themes, horses, mermaids, pelicans, penguins, and even chinchillas and hedgehogs, among many others, including Bettina's insects. You will also note that Bettina and Michelle's love for the environment reveals itself in their descriptions of some of their designs, such as the Tasmanian wolf, which has been extinct since 1936.

Bettina von Walhof vintage and now contemporary von Walhof Creations rhinestone jewelry is made to last, and will be the heirloom jewelry we pass down to our grandchildren.

This handmade Bettina von Walhof lobster pin must be seen to be believed. It measures a whopping 7¾" and the arms, legs, and antenna seem to bob along. It has prong set reddish-orange rhinestones all over the body and black stones for the eyes. **$1,200.00 – 1,300.00.** Barbara Wood collection.

Front view of lobster. This photo shows some of the dimension of this astonishing brooch.

Boop-boop-a-doop! Here is Bettina's Betty Boop showing off her little red outfit. **$1,100.00 – 1,200.00.** Betty Willson collection.

31

Bettina von Walhof Wicked Witch pin has three tremblers for lots of movement. The pin is 6½" x 4" and is signed. **$750.00 – 950.00.** Barbara Wood collection.

This blond rabbit by Bettina von Walhof with the red nose comes bearing gifts. His head is a trembler and he is 4" tall. **$350.00 – 400.00.** Barbara Wood collection.

This dashing red fox is another Bettina von Walhof creation and he also has a trembler head. The pin is 4" tall. **$300.00 – 350.00.** Barbara Wood collection.

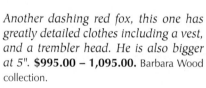

Another dashing red fox, this one has greatly detailed clothes including a vest, and a trembler head. He is also bigger at 5". **$995.00 – 1,095.00.** Barbara Wood collection.

This Bettina von Walhof black and white cat pin has lovely green eyes. 3½" x 2". **$350.00 – 400.00.** Barbara Wood collection.

This blue ladybug with trembler wings measures 2¼". Note that the legs are prong set black rhinestones. **$395.00 – 425.00.** Barbara Wood collection.

This Bettina von Walhof bunny is nearly identical to the bunny at left but he is much taller at 6½" . He is from a limited edition of only six. **$1,000.00 – 1,200.00.** Barbara Wood collection.

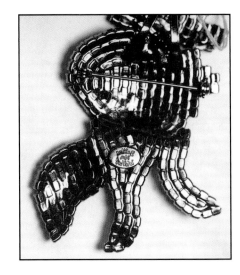

Reverse photo showing signature plaque.

Bettina von Walhof tassel owl pin, 4½" tall. **$225.00 – 250.00.** Barbara Wood collection.

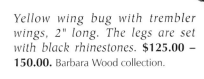

Yellow wing bug with trembler wings, 2" long. The legs are set with black rhinestones. **$125.00 – 150.00.** Barbara Wood collection.

Green wing bug with trembler wings, 2" long. **$125.00 – 150.00.** Barbara Wood collection.

This playful von Walhof kitten shows his love for you with his enormous heart. The kitten is pavé covered with red and black rhinestones, green eye accents, and of course, a little red mouth to go with his big red heart. This pin is signed "B & M von Walhof" for Bettina and Michelle von Walhof. The pin is nearly 4" tall and is 2½" wide. **$325.00 – 375.00.** Barbara Wood collection.

Reverse view showing signature heart plaque.

Bettina von Walhof red and clear flower pin with japanned back. The pin is 4⅝" tall and the flower is over 2" wide. **$225.00 – 250.00.** Barbara Wood collection.

Reverse view showing signature.

Eisenberg

This Eisenberg Original Sterling fur clip in a leaf design has clear, pink and purple rhinestones. It is 3½" x 2¾". **$650.00 – 750.00.** Carol Bell Treasures-In-Time collection.

Eisenberg is a name well known to all costume jewelry collectors. They started out as a clothing manufacturer, and gave ladies that little something extra, a lovely brooch attached right to the dress. But here is a story you may not have heard about Eisenberg.

Oreste Agnini was born in Naples, Italy, in 1885. He and his partner Ralph Singer, founded the costume jewelry company of Agnini & Singer in Chicago, Illinois, in 1921. They later changed the name of the company to ORA. Now comes the interesting story as told by Joanne Dubbs Ball and Dorothy Hehl Torem in *Masterpieces of Costume Jewelry*.

"It was Agnini & Singer who were responsible for supplying many of the buttons, pins, and brooches that were so coveted on Eisenberg dresses prior to the formation of the Eisenberg jewelry operation," Ball and Torem relate. That's right, the brooches so coveted that they were stolen right off the dress were not made by Eisenberg, in the beginning. But the Eisenbergs knew a good thing when they saw it, or heard it rather. When the thefts were reported to them, Eisenberg Jewelry, Inc., was born.

Eisenberg used several marks, helping collectors to date their jewelry. The Eisenberg Original wonderful large clips and pins manufactured from the 1930s to the pre-war 1940s were marked "Sterling" or "Sterling" with a script "E" or "Eisenberg Original Sterling," according to *Costume Jewelers, The Golden Age of Design* by Joanne Dubbs Ball.

"Eisenberg" in block letters was used from 1945 to 1950. "Eisenberg" in small block letters on a marker was used in the 1950s. Ball further states that "Eisenberg Ice" was used from 1960 to the present. "Eisenberg Ice" in script was used only in advertising and packaging.

Eisenberg has taken a down turn in value recently due to fakes and reproductions. Only the very best Eisenberg is bringing the high prices it once commanded. It is an excellent time for collectors to acquire Eisenberg, as prices should balance out in time due to the quality of manufacturing and stones.

In recent years, Eisenberg has turned their manufacturing to Christmas tree pins, bringing back many of their older designs. The marks read "EISENBERG ICE," and many are on cards reading the same, in script. There were also small gray boxes with "Eisenberg Ice" in script on the top. Earrings too small to mark were on cards with the mark in script.

All of their designs are attractive, but the tree with elongated emerald green marquise stones for the entire tree is perhaps the prettiest. The tree stand is made of clear round rhinestones, and the gold star top sports a large round red rhinestone. This tree sells for anywhere from $45.00 to $65.00, and up, when you can find it. Another great design is the fat little gold tree with gold balls and rhinestones scattered about the tree and a larger stone in the top. This style tree came in a variety of color combinations, including mixed, all clears, and all blues, in gold tone and silver tone.

Eisenberg will remain a perennial favorite due to design and quality, past and present. Hopefully they will begin making their lovely brooches again soon.

About the recast Eisenberg jewelry: This jewelry is *not* made by Eisenberg; it is made by someone who is recasting the jewelry and selling it. It is sold by the recaster as recast jewelry, with a price reflecting that it is a recast. Prices are still high, up to $200.00, but if you like the design, and believe it is a good price, you should buy it. Just remember, it will not go up in value the way a genuine Eisenberg piece would. And of course the problem comes when the piece is next sold. Or sold the time after that one. When it gets away from the person who recast it and sold it, it may never again be called recast except by an honest dealer.

The worst thing about recast jewelry is that it brings the value down for the genuine pieces, since most collectors are unable to tell the difference without some intense education, and many collectors have turned away from Eisenberg, and other companies whose jewelry is being recast. The best thing about it is that you may be able to add a dreamed of piece to your collection that is completely unavailable, and most of the time is much more affordable.

The recast Eisenberg jewelry is shown to give you some idea of what these pieces look like, including any marks. Education is your best protector against fakes, and there are now many websites whose owners willingly educate collectors about the fakes, reproductions, and recasts. Buy with care.

Note: This column was written several years ago, and to my great delight, Eisenberg has indeed started making jewelry besides Christmas tree designs. My friend Bobye Syverson, who is the pre-eminent Eisenberg specialist, told me that Eisenberg has started making some small figurals, some of the designs from their Classic line, some pins, a few necklaces, and some earrings. The pieces from the Classics line are the ones they issued in 1994 and in 2000, bringing the bestsellers back. The Classics designs are from the 1940s and 1950s lines. This is beautiful jewelry that will continue to become heirlooms. Thank you, Eisenberg.

This Eisenberg Original fur clip has an antique gold finish. It is covered with red, green, and clear rhinestones. The clip is 3" x 2¾". **$350.00 – 400.00.** Carol Bell Treasures-In-Time collection.

This Eisenberg Original fur clip is a stylized bird, with red and green cabochons. The clip is 4" x 2½". **$325.00 – 375.00.** Carol Bell Treasures-In-Time collection.

This Eisenberg Sterling floral fur clip is glorious with different colored and shaped rhinestones. The clip is 4" x 2¾". **$600.00 – 650.00.** Carol Bell Treasures-In-Time collection.

This Eisenberg Sterling floral fur clip has rose pink and clear rhinestones. The clip is 4½" x 2½". **$800.00 – 900.00.** Carol Bell Treasures-In-Time collection.

Here is a fabulous pair of Eisenberg Original Sterling fur clips with clear and dark green rhinestones. Both clips are signed and are 1⅝" x 1⅜". **$450.00 – 500.00.** Carol Bell Treasures-In-Time collection.

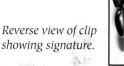

Reverse view of clip showing signature.

This is an Eisenberg fur clip/pin you can only appreciate in person. It has bright orange glass beads and clear rhinestones. It is 1½" x ¾". **$100.00 – 125.00.** Carol Bell Treasures-In-Time collection.

This Eisenberg fur clip is signed with a script "E" on the back, 1¼" x 1⅛". **$195.00 – 225.00.** Carol Bell Treasures-In-Time collection.

This Eisenberg Ice pale green and clear rhinestone pin is a wonderful example of Eisenberg design. The pin is 2⅜" x 1⅜" and is marked "Eisenberg Ice" in upper case block letters beside the copyright symbol. **$100.00 – 125.00.** Author collection.

This Eisenberg Ice clear rhinestone pin with large prong set round and marquise stones accented with glued in stones is 2¼" x 1¾" and is signed "© Eisenberg Ice." **$125.00 – 150.00.** Author collection.

This Eisenberg Ice pin with clear rhinestones is signed "© Eisenberg Ice" and is 2⅜" x 1¼". **$100.00 – 125.00.** Author collection.

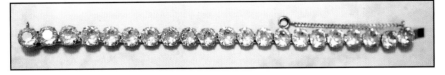

This Eisenberg bracelet with large clear rhinestones is 7⅛" long and has a push-in clasp that virtually disappears when closed. The bracelet has a safety chain and is signed "Eisenberg" in block letters. **$125.00 – 150.00.** Author collection.

This Eisenberg bracelet with two rows of clear oval and emerald shaped rhinestones has a safety chain, is signed "Eisenberg" on the back of the push-in clasp and is 7¼" x ½". **$175.00 – 225.00.** Author collection.

This Eisenberg bracelet has two rows of clear marquise rhinestones accented with clear round stones, signed, and is 7" x 1". This bracelet features the hidden clasp where it becomes part of the design. **$175.00 – 225.00.** Author collection.

This Eisenberg bracelet with one row of large clear rhinestones accented with little rhinestone filled accent designs is 7" long and is signed. **$150.00 – 175.00.** Author collection.

This most beautiful and rare Eisenberg bracelet in gold-tone setting has two rows of prong set clear rhinestones accented with the tiny rhinestone swirls atop the large stones. It has a hidden push-in clasp, is signed "Eisenberg" in script lettering, and is 7¼" long. **$400.00 – 500.00.** Author collection.

These ¾" Eisenberg emerald green and clear rhinestone clip-on earrings are marked on the back with the script E. **$35.00 – 55.00.** Author collection

Classically beautiful Eisenberg ring with small stones surrounding a larger stone. It is a size 8 and has the script E inside along with part of the Eisenberg signature. **$325.00 – 375.00.** Carol Bell Treasures-In-Time collection.

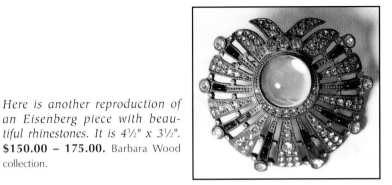

Here is another reproduction of an Eisenberg piece with beautiful rhinestones. It is 4½" x 3½". **$150.00 – 175.00.** Barbara Wood collection.

Reverse view showing mark.

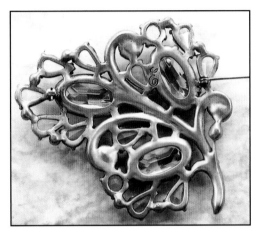

This recast of an Eisenberg pin has lovely clear stones and large AB oval stones, which are open backed. It is signed with the script "E" and is 3¼" x 2⅝". **$155.00 – 175.00.** Barbara Wood collection.

Reverse view.

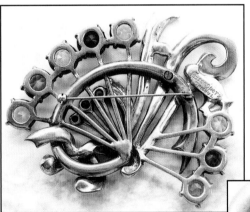

Reverse view of Eisenberg recast showing signature.

Recast of an Eisenberg Original pin with clear rhinestones accenting round colored unfoiled glass stones. Those colored stones and the three small cabochon stones are open backed. It is made of two pieces that have been screwed together and is signed "Eisenberg Original." It is 3½" x 3". **$175.00 – 200.00.** Barbara Wood collection.

Close up-view of mark.

Suzanne Bjontegard

A few years ago when searching online for some fruit jewelry, I came across a sweet little rhinestone pear pin. It came in its original box and the pin itself was signed "SUZANNE BJØNTEGÅRD." Over the years I have added quite a few more pieces to my collection, as you will see.

I adore this jewelry. It has everything that speaks to my personal collecting muse — bold use of rhinestones, over the top designs, cheerful, fun, and fruity! It is all quite solid and well made, and I wear it more frequently than any other in my jewelry collection.

Here is the double cherries pin which has red rhinestones on the cherries and AB rhinestones on the leaves. It is signed and is 1½" x 1⅝". $165.00 – 185.00. Author collection.

I have found three different signatures for this designer. First is "Suzanne Bjontegard," spelled out in all caps. Second is the block letters "S.B." This mark is usually found on small things like the tiny fruit pins with tie tack backs. Last is the fancy script "SB," which looks like the "SB" on top of her black boxes.

My research has found a little information about this designer. She originally sold jewelry through the Home Shopping Network. Later she sold jewelry through the QVC shopping network in England. I found a link to a website but it is no longer available. In fact, nearly every link I click on for information about her no longer exists.

What little I have found seems to be that she is/was a British fashion designer/celebrity who owned/owns several boutiques and who made jewelry lines for the two shopping networks previously mentioned, and later for something called ShoppingTelly.com. Her beautiful and well made designs came in black boxes with her name and a card enclosed telling you how to care for the jewelry. Her jewelry line was called California Style.

Her next line saw a complete turn around in design, going very simple with quiet muted designs. Her boxes changed to lavender and say Suzi B. This line has none of the punch and life of the previous line.

Her early jewelry could be considered rare, as the good designs are not easily found. I must admit to being a somewhat greedy collector. I have three of her purple grapes pin/pendants and three of her green grapes pin/pendants. I also have three of her blue pocketbook pins and only one pink one. So far. Oh, and two flamingo pins. But who could resist those?

Bjontegard hummingbird pin in red, blue, green, and clear rhinestones with a blue stone eye. It is signed and is 2¾" x 2⅜". $75.00 – 95.00. Author collection.

This pin is a gorgeous and tasty strawberry with black seeds with a built-in bale to allow you to wear it as a pendant. It is signed and is 1¾" tall. $165.00 – 185.00. Author collection.

Here is the strawberry scatter pin alongside the pineapple scatter pin. Both are signed "SB" and are over 1" tall. $25.00 – 35.00 each. Author collection.

This apple with the single bite out of it came in two sizes. This larger one is covered with red stones and has clear ones marking the bite. There is a bale that can be attached to allow you to add it to a chain. The pin is signed and is 1¾" x 1⅝". $165.00 – 185.00. Author collection.

Reverse view of apple showing signature.

Here is the smaller apple, which has AB stones in the bite. It is signed and is 1¼" x 1½". This apple came with a uniquely designed bale which allows it to be worn as a pendant. **$125.00 – 150.00.** Author collection.

This apple scatter pin is signed and is ⅞" x ⅞". **$25.00 – 35.00.** Author collection.

All three size apples shown together.

Reverse view of middle apple with bale.

View of apple with bale attached to the chain.

I am crazy for these grape pins, they have an attached bale so you can wear them on a chain, which some of them come with, or perhaps sellers keep them since they are so nice. This grape pin has dark purple stones and AB stones on the leaves. It is signed and is 2⅛" tall. **$165.00 – 185.00.** Author collection.

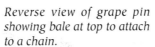

Reverse view of grape pin showing bale at top to attach to a chain.

This grape pin/pendant has its original chain and is almost the same as the previous one, but this one has clear AB stones as highlights on each grape. How much fun is that? **$165.00 – 185.00.** Author collection.

Here is the same grape design, rendered in green. This pin/pendant is signed and is 2⅛" tall. **$165.00 – 185.00.** Author collection.

And here again is the grape pin/pendant with highlights. I love to wear these grapes. I usually wear the purple grape necklace and the green grape pin; it is a good look. This one is signed and has its own chain. **$165.00 – 185.00.** Author collection.

Green grape pin/pendants shown together to show the difference in the stones. The one on right has AB highlight stones.

Here is a pear with a bite out to match your apples. A bale can be attached so this can be worn on a chain. This pin is signed and is 2" x 1". **$125.00 – 150.00.** Author collection.

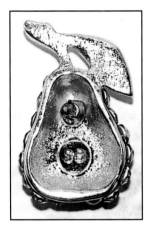

Here are a pair of pear scatter pins, both are signed "SB." They are 1" tall. **$95.00 – 125.00.** Author collection.

Reverse view of pear scatter pin showing SB signature.

Then you would need a pair of matching earrings, one of which is signed. Note the stem and leaf go different ways, a nice design touch. They are 1" tall. **$65.00 – 75.00.** Author collection.

This flamingo is another of my favorites, it is oversized and extremely gaudy. This pin has enameling, pink rhinestones on the body, and a green stone eye. It is signed and stands 3¾" tall. **$125.00 – 150.00.** Author collection.

Here is a vase filled with flowers and all of the pink and green rhinestones are prong set. This signed pin is weighty, as is all of this jewelry. This pin is 2¾" x 2". **$95.00 – 125.00.** Author collection.

Since this pin is so small, there is probably a larger version around somewhere. This little blue dolphin with the red eye is 2" long and is signed. **$65.00 – 75.00.** Author collection.

Reverse view of dolphin showing signature.

This sweet little blue pocket-book with AB stones is signed and almost 2" tall. **$65.00 – 75.00.** Author collection.

Same little pocketbook in pink with AB stones. **$65.00 – 75.00.** Author collection.

This apple pin in red AB stones is signed with the same swirly "SB" that the watches are signed with, but they are from a different design line. It is 2¼" x 1⅞". **$95.00 – 125.00.** Author collection.

Reverse view of the apple pin showing SB signature at top left.

The apple pin in green is not signed but is identical to the red one. **$95.00 – 125.00.** Author collection.

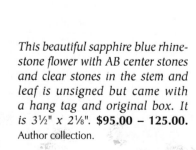

This beautiful sapphire blue rhinestone flower with AB center stones and clear stones in the stem and leaf is unsigned but came with a hang tag and original box. It is 3½" x 2⅛". **$95.00 – 125.00.** Author collection.

This sapphire blue hot air balloon came in the box with the hang tag but is not signed. It is 2" tall. **$65.00 – 85.00.** Author collection.

Here is a beautiful rendition of a leopard with black spots and green eyes and a red mouth. He looks perfect perched atop a shoulder. It is signed Suzanne Bjontegard, as are most of her pieces that are big enough to hold her signature. This pin is nearly 4" long. **$100.00 – 125.00.** Author collection.

This large Bjontegard turtle pin with large black eyes is the exact shape and size of a small turtle. It is signed and is 2⅜" long and 1⅞" wide, and ¾" tall. **$85.00 – 115.00.** Author collection.

This beautiful bracelet uses clear, AB, and opaque stones in a floral design. It has a hang tag and is 7½". **$100.00 – 125.00.** Author collection.

This necklace has olive green glass beads and rhinestone beads. It has a hang tag and is 35" long. **$100.00 – 125.00.** Author collection.

This ruby red bracelet is not signed but it came in the original box with the paper hang tag attached. It has two rows of square red stones and it is 7½" long. **$65.00 – 95.00.** Author collection.

This bracelet is also unsigned but also came in its original box with the paper hang tag. All the rhinestones are prong set. It is 7" long. **$65.00 – 95.00.** Author collection.

These lively green earrings came on the original card but are not signed. They are clip-ons and measure 1¾" long. **$45.00 – 65.00.** Author collection.

This bracelet came in a special size box for Suzanne Bjontegard but the bracelet itself is not marked. It is purple Lucite with amethyst stones and is ⅞" wide. **$55.00 – 75.00.** Author collection.

Fruit, Vegetables, and Fruit Salad

I continue my search for fruit and vegetable jewelry, but it is a very tough category to collect, because there are many other collectors competing for the same pieces. The prices of Forbidden Fruit jewelry continues to rise, as does any piece of Bakelite fruit jewelry and true fruit salad jewelry. Still, I continue to be amused by any piece of fruit or vegetable jewelry, whether it is a $1.00 piece or a $100.00 piece.

More fruit and vegetable jewelry can be found in the chapter on Artful Plastics and Suzanne Bjontegard, and vintage fruit beads can be found in the Contemporary chapter with the jewelry of Annie Navetta.

Only one word can describe this Butler & Wilson fruit cuff bracelet — stupendous. I took twenty photographs of this bracelet and not one came close to capturing its fun and beauty. It is an amazing mix of colors with all types of fruit rendered: strawberries, apples, grapes, pears, cherries, and berries. The tiny gold-tone bee resides at the front edge of the cuff next to the orange strawberry. It is signed on a signature plaque inside the apple. **$175.00 – 250.00.** *Author collection.*

This celluloid bracelet with glass oranges and orange blossoms is 7" long. **$150.00 – 195.00.** *Author collection.*

These forbidden Fruit matched pins each hold a variety of rhinestone colors. They measure 1⅛" tall. **$125.00 – 150.00.** *Author collection.*

These forbidden Fruit apple juice colored Lucite with embedded magenta rhinestones earrings are 1" tall. **$75.00 – 100.00.** *Author collection.*

Reverse view of pin.

Extremely rare Forbidden Fruit corn with multicolored rhinestones. It is 2¼" tall. **$150.00+.** *Author collection.*

49

Forbidden Fruit grape pin with opaque pink Lucite and white rhinestones and Forbidden Fruit grape pin with opaque white Lucite and pale green rhinestones. They are nearly 2" tall. **$100.00 – 150.00 each.** Author collection.

Forbidden Fruit lemon pin with enameled leaves in lemony Lucite with lemony rhinestones and Forbidden Fruit lime with pale apple juice Lucite with an extremely pale green tint and pale green rhinestones. They are nearly 2" tall. **$100.00 – 150.00.** Author collection.

Forbidden Fruit Concord grape earrings in blue Lucite and Forbidden Fruit red grape pin with embedded ruby red rhinestones. (Only one earring is pictured to show that the pin and the earrings are the exact same size.) The earrings are 1¼" tall and are hard to find. **$65.00 – 105.00.** Author collection.

Fabulous pair of Forbidden Fruit grape earrings in orange with orange rhinestones. The color is actually a bright orange. They are 1¼" tall and are hard to find. **$65.00 – 105.00.** Author collection.

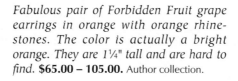  

Hong Kong pineapple necklace in orange and green. This necklace is the same design as the one in my first book. It is signed and is 26" with a 2¾" pineapple pendant drop. **$15.00 – 25.00.** Author collection.

Here are the matching earrings which are both signed. They dangle 2". **$5.00 – 10.00.** Author collection.

Here is the matching bracelet which is not signed. It is elastic to fit nearly every wrist. These are very lightweight plastic. **$20.00 – 30.00.** Author collection.

Here is the white pineapple beaded necklace that is not signed and is 48" long. **$20.00 – 30.00.** Author collection.

Matching white pineapple elastic bracelet. **$20.00 – 30.00.** Author collection.

This Venetian glass beaded necklace has green leaves and bananas. It is 17½" long. It is great design, especially for fruit jewelry lovers. **$150.00 – 175.00.** Author collection.

This pair of pears signed "Made in West Germany" is 2½" x 1½". **$65.00 – 75.00.** Barbara Wood collection.

Enameled and pavé pears fur clip. There are no visible markings but it could be Coro or Trifari. It measures 1¾" x 1⅜". **$95.00 – 125.00.** Author collection.

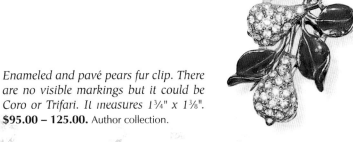

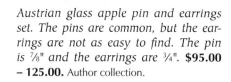

Austrian glass apple pin and earrings set. The pins are common, but the earrings are not as easy to find. The pin is ⅞" and the earrings are ¾". **$95.00 – 125.00.** Author collection.

There's nothing like a great big carrot pin perched on your lapel for Easter. Or when you are dieting and want to warn enablers away. This great unsigned pin in orange and green enameling has a couple of tiny dings but is still a great pin. It measures 4⅝" tall. **$95.00 – 115.00.** Author collection.

Austrian givré fruit pin with a glass stone of blue and purple. It is 1½" and signed "Austria." **$95.00 – 125.00.** Author collection.

Austrian givré peaches pin with glass fruit and glass leaves, accented with a pink rhinestone. It is 2" long. **$95.00 – 125.00.** Author collection.

Austrian red raspberries fruit pin with glass stones. It is 2½" and signed "Austria." **$95.00 – 125.00.** Author collection.

If you didn't look closely at these earrings, you would miss the Weiss mark that is inside the strawberry behind the ear clip. These great strawberry earrings are covered with red and green rhinestones in a japanned setting. Only one earring is marked. They are almost 1" tall. **$75.00 – 95.00.** Author collection.

BSK cherries rhinestone and enameled pin in japanned setting. It is 1¾" tall. $95.00 – 150.00. Author collection.

Another BSK fruit pin, this time with what appear to be red carrots in a japanned setting. It is 2¼" tall. $150.00 – 195.00. Author collection.

An unusual find of Vogue hair clips on their original card. Note the zip code in the address. Zip codes were first used in July 1963 so this lovely set of miniature fruits dates after that time. The clips appear to be in unworn condition. The fruit design on each clip is 2½" tall. $75.00 – 95.00. Author collection.

These ART blooming oranges earrings have enameled flowers and leaves. Only one earring is signed. They are 1" tall. $45.00 – 65.00. Author collection.

Hollycraft orange earrings with light and dark orange rhinestones and enameled leaves and flowers in a japanned setting. They are 1" tall. $55.00 – 75.00. Author collection.

This stylistic fruit bracelet is mounted on wire making it easily fit any wrist. The fruits are individually wired onto a glass beaded base. Look closely to see lemons, strawberries, and bananas, among others. $125.00 – 145.00. Author collection.

Original by Robert enameled tomato pin from his line of fruit and vegetable jewelry. It is 1¾" x 1½". **$65.00 – 85.00.** Author collection.

This unsigned apple pin has foiled opaque green stones that are set in an open back. It is 1¼" x 1¼". **$45.00 – 55.00.** Author collection.

Pair of Austrian berry fruit scatter pins with purple and green givré glass stones. They are 1¼" tall. **$95.00 – 125.00.** Author collection.

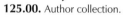

Reverse view of pins.

Pair of Austrian fruit pear scatter pins with green and brown givré glass stones. They are 1¼" tall. **$95.00 – 125.00.** Author collection.

Hard-to-find Austrian apple earrings with glass fruit and leaf stones accented with a small green rhinestone. Earrings are 1¼" tall and marked "Austria" on the ear clip. **$95.00 – 125.00.** Author collection.

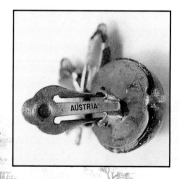

Reverse view of earring showing signature.

Pair of Austrian glass leaf earrings to match fruit pins. They are 1¼" and signed "Austria" on the ear clips. **$55.00 – 75.00.** Author collection.

Austrian apple pin with glass apples and leaves. It is 2¼" wide and signed "Austria" on the back of one apple. **$100.00 – 125.00.** Author collection.

This enameled lemon is from the Coro line of fruit designs. It is 2½" tall. **$85.00 – 115.00.** Author collection.

I love this set of Lucite strawberries. I believe they are from the 1970s. The big one was probably a necklace, the medium one a bracelet, and the small one part of an earring, but the last owner for some reason wanted them disconnected. However, since it is a simple matter to add a chain to the large one and to add the medium and small one to a charm bracelet, I had to have them anyway. The large berry is 2¾" tall and 1¾" wide, the medium berry is 1½" tall, and the small berry is ⅞" tall. **$65.00 – 85.00 for the set.** Author collection.

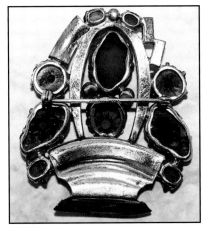

This is one of those pieces of jewelry I can't wear around other collectors; they all want to buy it right off of me. It has what looks like poured glass fruit and fruit salad stones with clear rhinestones. This silver-tone pin is unsigned. It is 1¾" x 2" and the fruit salad stones have an open back. **$125.00 – 150.00.** Author collection.

Reverse view of fruit salad pin.

Unsigned fruit salad pin with pink glass fruit stones. The setting is open behind pink stones. It is 1¼" in diameter. **$100.00 – 145.00.** Author collection.

Great reddish orange bananas bracelet strung on elastic. The bananas are 1⅝" long. **$45.00 – 55.00.** Author collection.

This beautiful ruby red fruit salad pin is unmarked but judging from the back of the pin, it could be either Mazer or Trifari. It is 1⅝" x 1⅜" long. **$100.00 – 150.00.** Author collection.

This wonderful fruit salad bracelet is unsigned but looks like Mazer or Trifari. It has red, green, and blue glass flowers and is accented with clear rhinestones. It is 7" long. **$150.00 – 200.00.** Author collection.

Another gorgeous unsigned fruit salad bracelet with sapphire blue flowers accented with clear stones. It is 7" long. **$150.00 – 200.00.** Author collection.

Unsigned bracelet with blue and white fruit salad plastic stones accented with rhinestones. It is 7½" long. **$45.00 – 75.00.** Author collection.

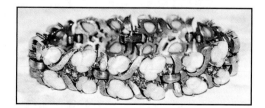

Trifari fruit salad bracelet with white fruits in a gold-tone setting accented with pink AB stones. It is signed and 7" long. **$145.00 – 165.00.** Author collection.

fur Clips, Dress Clips, and Shoe Clips

One of the most consistently expensive items of vintage costume jewelry continues to be fur clips. Fur clips were more costly when originally manufactured, and some of them remain on the "must have" list for collectors everywhere. Many of the famous Coro designs for the Coro duettes are fur clips made into an interchangeable brooch with the duette mechanism. All of the big companies made fur clips, such as Mazer, Trifari, De Rosa, Reinad, Reja, and Eisenberg. And of course many are unsigned.

These fur clips were usually substantial pieces of jewelry because they had to go through the fur and the liner in order to be attached to the fur. To do this, fur clips normally had two prongs to make insertion easier. Some fur clips boast an extra safety catch to fasten after the clip has been inserted through the fur. Fur clips are available in every price range from a few dollars to more than a thousand dollars.

Hobé gilt fur clip with red, blue, and clear rhinestones. It is signed on the back in a signature plaque. The clip is 2¼" x 1½". $275.00 – 300.00. Carol Bell Treasures-In-Time collection.

Dress clips differ from fur clips in that they have a flat flip-up clip that allows them to be attached to clothing in a corner such as a boat neck top or on any flat edge of the clothing. The clips usually, but not always, have little teeth on the sides and end to help them grip. Many duettes from different companies are a pair of dress clips. The Trifari duette pins were called Clip Mates. Duettes with dress clips were very versatile because you could turn one pin into two. Duette clips could be worn in places besides the lapel area. They could be pinned to a hat, or the front of a belt mimicking a buckle, on sleeves like cuff links, pretty much anywhere a woman could place them and know they would hold.

Shoe clips, while working on the same design as dress clips, are nevertheless different. They have small fasteners to allow them to be clipped to shoes, either on the top or in some cases on the back of the shoe. Certain designs of shoes lend the clips to being placed on the upper side of a shoe. These clips are usually very small, with a tooth or two to hold onto the shoe. Most cannot be attached to clothing because the fastener is very short, especially the larger clips, whose weight would cause them to fall right off of a shirt or blouse.

One problem with collecting these clips is the search for them, because many sellers and dealers incorrectly believe them to be interchangeable, and call them fur/dress/shoe clips. They also call dress or shoe clips simply fur clips. One reason is that most fur clips will sell for more than dress clips and much more than shoe clips. I recently sent out a request for information to some sellers of fur clips that were actually dress or shoe clips and asked them how I would attach the said clip to my fur. Many of the responses were downright comical, out of 20 queries, only one admitted that they didn't know. This seller also offered to research it for me to find the answer. Many sellers were actually curt to the point of being rude; two said "just look at the picture." I did, they were both dress clips. If you look at the photos accompanying this column, you will see that while it may be possible to attach a dress clip to a fur coat or jacket, it could only be worn along the edge of the fur; this is not the original intention.

Sellers were very creative in trying to figure out how to explain how to attach the clip in their quest for my business. One said you would use the clip to hold two pieces of fur together, such as a stole. Another said the teeth "grab hold of the fur and hold on." Another said you would "just open it up to grab some fur and slap it closed."

While this was quite amusing, it was no help in finding fur clips to purchase. Unless the seller or dealer shows the back of the clip, or the prongs are visible beneath the clip, collectors will need to familiarize themselves with the basic designs of desired fur clips. The best places to go for this information is books and the bigger vintage costume jewelry websites. Because the authors know the difference and are actually handling the fur clips, you can be assured they will have the clip correctly labeled. Fur clips are still a wonderful piece of jewelry to own and wear, even if you don't have a fur coat to wear them on. The prongs allow them to be attached to almost any clothing except for very thin or lightweight fabric. Fur clips look wonderful on jackets or winter coats. They can even be worn with shirts or sweaters by anchoring them to an undergarment strap. And some-

Here is the fantastic Coro Craft Sterling birds duette. The enameled pair of birds have leaves and flower accents. The duette frame is marked "Coro Duette Sterling Pat. No. 1798867." $350.00 – 395.00. Carol Bell Treasures-In-Time collection.

times they can be found for remarkable bargain prices because few people actively seek them. Designs for fur clips include flowers, animals, birds, fish, and even people. Look to add some to your collection.

Note: More dress clips can be seen in the Artful Plastics chapter.

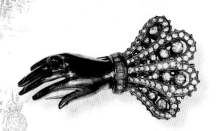

Trifari hand fur clip with elaborate sleeve cuff in sterling. It has the crown Trifari mark and is 2" long. **$175.00 – 200.00.** Carol Bell Treasures-In-Time collection.

This colorful enameled bird is the unmarked half of a Coro Craft Sterling duette of birds with flowers. Each piece is different as they were hand enameled and the painting differs slightly on each. It is 2" long and the clip itself is marked "Sterling." **$50.00 – 85.00.** Author collection.

Here is a matching pair of angel fish fur clips, mother and baby. I have seen this pair with the duette and I believe they are unmarked Coro. Many times the Coro duettes were marked on the frame and not on the fur clips themselves. The clips feature white, yellow, and orange enameling with green rhinestone eyes. Mom is 1⅞" x 1⅝" and baby is 1" x 1⅜". **$100.00 – 150.00.** Author collection.

Coro apple blossom flowered duettes from 1948 with enameling and scattered rhinestones, fur clips measure 2" x 1¼". **$95.00 – 150.00.** Author collection.

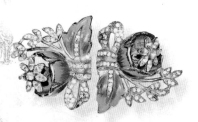

Pair of unsigned Coro duette flower dress clips, gold tone, enameled with clear rhinestones. The flowers inside the blossom tremble. Each clip is 1⅝" x 1½". **$85.00 – 115.00.** Author collection.

Another pair of unsigned Coro duette flower dress clips, silver tone, enameled with clear and blue rhinestones. Note this set is the same set as the previous one, but the rhinestones and the trembler flower are different. Also, this pair has emerald cut blue rhinestones where the previous pair has only enameling. Same size. **$85.00 – 115.00.** Author collection.

Reverse view of dress clip.

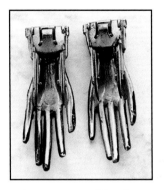

Unsigned fur clip with trembler flower, very similar to Coro designs, with rhinestones and enameling. It is 2⅛" long. **$75.00 – 95.00.** Author collection.

I believe this pair of hand fur clips is wearing black gloves, because there is gold decoration on the cuffs. But I could be wrong. Each hand is over 1½" long and neither is marked, they could be a duette or a clip mate without a frame. **$125.00 – 150.00.** Author collection.

Reverse view of fur clips.

This fur clip may be in poor condition but he still retains his personality. He appears to be an accordion player. This pot metal fur clip is not signed but could be from the Trifari line of figural fur clips. It is 1¾" tall. **$45.00 – 65.00.** Author collection.

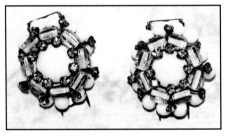

Pair of milk glass fur clips with clear beads and clear rhinestones. Neither is signed. Each clip is 1⅛" in diameter. **$75.00 – 95.00.** Author collection.

I believe this fur clip is part of a Coro duette and is missing its mate. It is enameled and the body has pavé rhinestones, and one little red stone eye. It is 1¾" wide. **$75.00 – 95.00.** Author collection.

This dark pink moonglow set has a chatelaine that has a pin back on the bow and the other part is a fur clip. None of the pieces are signed but it could be Richelieu. The chain is 6½" long, the bow is 1½", and the clip is 1¼" in diameter. The earrings are 1" tall. **$65.00 – 85.00.** Author collection.

59

Coro moonstone enameled and rhinestone fur clip with pale pink cabochons. It is 2¾" and is signed. **$95.00 – 125.00.** Author collection.

Marcel Boucher fur clip with the Phrygian cap mark and the number "2835" on the back. It has clear rhinestones and is 1⅝" x 1½". **$95.00 – 125.00.** Author collection.

Reverse view of clip.

Beautiful clear rhinestones fur clip with prong set stones. It is unsigned but could be part of a Trifari clip mate. It is 1⅝" tall. **$65.00 – 80.00.** Author collection.

Here is a stunning pair of unsigned Schreiner fur clips with prong set stones in green and blue. They could be some type of fruit or berry because there is a large blue glass cabochon mounted behind the rhinestones, which are foiled and open backed. They are 1½". Each has one green and one blue leaf stone. **$150.00 – 175.00.** Author collection.

Here is a beautiful Monet dress clip. It is marked "Monet" and "Pat. 1852188," I think, it is hard to see as it is stamped on a curve. This lovely dress clip has tiny colored glass cabochons in elaborate prongs. Note the dress clip has a spring in the top center. **$45.00 – 55.00.** Author collection.

Stunning 1930s rhinestone dress clip with gorgeous ruby red unfoiled and open backed glass stones. It is 1¾" x 1¼". **$95.00 – 115.00.** Barbara Wood collection.

This is the Coro Craft Heavenly Swallows fur clip from 1944. It is also marked "Sterling." It is lovely even without its mate. **$65.00 – 95.00.** Author collection.

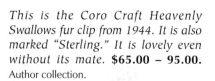

Made in Spain

One thing I always keep in mind when jewelry shopping is to look for something that is fun. One little pin that recently caught my eye in a showcase made me laugh out loud, and I knew it had to come home with me. It was a very small pin, of what is most likely a Japanese lady, with a colorful ribboned hat, glasses and a tiny camera hanging from her neck. She looks like a perfect little tourist, in her blue and white polka dotted sundress with matching blue shoes. She has a pearl cabochon head. The camera and strap are attached separately, like a genuine camera, and swing freely around her neck. She is very petite, less than two inches tall. I brought her home and she perches on the shelf of my computer hutch, and brings a smile to me every day.

The mark on the back of her head says "SPAIN." When I got her home, I realized I had a small collection of Spanish jewelry, all purchased because it fit the "fun" category. Most of the Spanish jewelry in my collection is damascene, which is a process where a soft metal, such as gold is inlaid into a harder metal, such as steel. It is a process believed to have been started centuries ago in the city of Damascus, but it is Toledo, Spain, that is now famous for their damascene artwork. Many of the subjects in damascene and Spanish jewelry are figurals, such as animals, insects, ships, fish and marine animals, musical instruments, and people. Some have moving parts such as a horse or donkey drawn cart with movable wheels.

This adorable little Japanese tourist lady has her camera around her neck like a necklace, allowing for its movement. This is one of my favorite figurals, she is so cute with her little ribboned bonnet and blue dress with matching shoes. She is signed "Spain" behind her head where it is difficult to see. She is 1¾" tall. $20.00 – 35.00. Author collection.

Some Spanish jewelry, such as the ones featuring stringed musical instruments like guitars, have plastic or Lucite faux mother of pearl as the body of the instrument, and a darker piece, such as orange, to show off the bridge, saddle, and actual strings of the piece of jewelry. Most of the strings I have seen are made of tiny strands of wire.

Spanish jewelry is very affordable, for the most part. Pins can be found for as little as $5.00 and as much as $80.00 to $100.00 for more intricate pieces. Bracelets are less common and usually start at $20.00 and go up. Damascene charm bracelets seem to be rare and are priced from $25.00 up. I would speculate that most of the Spanish jewelry sold secondhand was purchased as souvenirs. The jewelry is lovely with a rich gold tone mimicking genuine gold jewelry, but the prices allow collectors to build a sizeable, and fun, collection quickly and inexpensively.

Musical instrument made in Spain. Notice it has tiny individual strings attached. It is signed "Spain" and is 1¾" tall. $50.00 – 65.00. Author collection.

This spanish cat damascene pin has blue eyes. It is signed and is 2" tall. $10.00 – 20.00. Author collection.

This great Spanish bug pin has a large faux pearl body hidden under its wings. Its orange and blue colors are a bit unusual. It is signed "Spain" and is 2¼". $20.00 – 30.00. Author collection.

This blue set was purchased along with other souvenir jewelry from Spain from the same collector, but this set is not marked. The bracelet is 6½" and the earrings are for pierced ears. A lovely well made set. **$30.00 – 45.00.** Author collection.

This damascene charm bracelet is a great find. It is 7" long and has some great charms on it. **$25.00 – 45.00.** Author collection.

Kicking donkey pin by Arabesque of Spain. The pin is not signed but it is on the original card. It is 1½" long. **$15.00 – 25.00.** Author collection.

The Spanish dancer pin by Arabesque from Spain is not signed but is on its original card. It stands 1½" tall. **$15.00 – 25.00.** Author collection.

Charm Bracelets

Heavy silver-tone Napier charm style bracelet with a pair of blue Lucite moonstone beads below an elaborate design. It is 7" long and the charm drops are 1½". **$75.00 – 100.00.** Author collection.

An elderly gentleman asked me if I would like to see his wife's bracelet. She had passed away 11 years before, and he had just gotten it out of his safe deposit box to give to his son. His face lit up as he shared each charm's story with me. There was a rickshaw from the time they went to San Francisco, a policeman in Bermuda shorts from their visit to Bermuda, an Eiffel Tower from their trip to Paris. There was even a charm shaped like a ball that folded out to reveal tiny photographs of him and his sons. "My wife wore this bracelet every single day," he proudly proclaimed.

Charm bracelets have experienced a recent resurgence in popularity. There are two types of collectors; first, those who have one bracelet that has charms they and their family members have added for special occasions or special memories. Nancy Hathaway of Ormond Beach, Florida, used to collect charm bracelets because "I like the jingle!jangle!" she laughs, "but decided to start my own with charms that have a special meaning for me, like an ice cream cone, one that says Born To Shop, sea life, things like that. My husband loves apples so I have a glass apple charm, it's really cute. These are all in 14 kt. so I can wear it all the time, I call it my memory bracelet."

Molly Garza has a very special bracelet, well, part of a very special bracelet. It is a portion of her mother's sterling heart bracelet which she divided into two bracelets, one for each daughter. "I love it because the charms were from her friends, my grandparents, and relatives from the early 1940s," says Garza. "I think that charm bracelets are symbolic of one's little passions in life. Another of my favorites is my 14 kt. gold baby charm bracelet that holds my baby locket, my baby heart, and another enameled heart locket that was mine as a baby. They are separated by the silhouette heads of my son and daughter. I could go on and on about charm bracelets and how completely 'charming' they are to me," she concludes with a smile.

Then there are those collectors who are so charmed by these bracelets that they can't stop with just one, or two, or even three. "I have several dozen charm bracelets — most with a story," says Betty Spaulding of Signal Mountain, Tennessee. "My most favorite one is my States bracelet, I have all 50 states, with DC and the State of Confusion on *one* bracelet! It took me 10 years to accumulate it, and many of the members of JewelCollect (www. lizjewel.com) helped me with the last 10 or 12 that I needed. Yes, it weighs a *ton*, and I don't wear it all that much because people stop me in the street and grab my arm to look at it."

"Then I have collected some of the cities," Spaulding continues. "The old tourist-y ones, of New York and Chicago and San Francisco, etc. I have maybe eight of those. I have a travel one, with all sorts of travel-oriented symbols, and a Western one, with cowboys and boots and such. I even have a charm necklace, I took all the charms from my teenage bracelet, my mother's bracelet, my mother-in-law's, and my step-mother's sister, and put them on a chain to make a necklace. I love charm bracelets, especially the ones that obviously have a history about which I know nothing, but love to make up stories. I *love* charm bracelets," she concludes.

Napier Charm Bracelets

Another type of charm bracelet is manufactured with a theme, by companies such as Coro and Napier. Dealer and collector Cathy Gordon discovered Napier charm bracelets last year, and has been snapping up these beauties wherever and whenever she can find them. "I found them to be so unique with such a lot of detail that I started looking for them for myself. The first one I bought is the one with the colored Lucite fruits on it — I didn't know until later that it was missing the cherries!" she exclaims. "So then I had to find one with all the fruits! I have several with Asian themes, Buddhas, lotus flower coins, etc. I have the seashell one and a really unique one with four faces, each with a hat to represent the type — a Mountie, a Chinese person, a guy with a bowler, and a Cavalier with

This Napier bracelet came with the bell-like charm, and the owner added the Florida palm tree and the articulated lobster, both of which are 14 kt. gold. The bracelet is 7½" long with a textured finish and is marked on clasp. **$100.00 – 125.00.** Author collection.

Charm Bracelets

Here is one of my favorite Napier charm style bracelets. It is big and bold with great colors of Lucite beads. It is 7" long and is marked "Napier" on the clasp. The largest bead dangles are over 1" tall. **$150.00 – 200.00.** Author collection.

a feather. Very cute. I too love the jingley sounds, some even have bells. I also like the size and sheer outrageousness of them!" says Gordon. If you haven't gotten one yet, it's time to start. One of your grand-daughters will really appreciate it.

The popularity of Napier charm style bracelets has skyrocketed in the past year or so. The bracelets in high demand include those with an Oriental or Asian theme, the stylized fruit charm bracelet, and the bobbles bracelets. Napier was in business for most of the last century, but they originally began by making silverware products. Some of their products included piggy banks made to look like a variety of animals, even a cute little egg; breweriana such as cocktail shakers and jiggers; hors d'oeuvre holders such as a swan with a Bakelite bead head and tiny holes throughout its body allowing toothpicks holding little snacks to be inserted; and even some unusual vanity items such as jewelry holders.

One of my favorite vanity items is a bellhop or porter from the World's Fair of 1939. He is carrying two empty bags, one of which can hold a package of cigarettes and the other a box of matches. His head is also a round Bakelite bead. He is adorable but sells for between $50.00 and $100.00 when available for sale.

After a few name changes in the early years, the company settled on Napier around 1920, and after World War I they began concentrating on manufacturing costume jewelry. The bracelets currently commanding high prices from collectors were made mostly in the mid to late 1950s and the 1960s and even the 1970s. There is an amazing variety available for collectors.

Napier charm bracelets are signed in several different ways. One is the small fold-over clasp signed "Napier" on the back, the next is the large fold-over clasp also signed on the back. The most unusual is the large spring ring clasp with an extra bar inside the spring ring. This bent bar has the word "Napier" on it.

The glass elephant charm bracelets generally sell for between $150.00 and $200.00 or more, depending on condition. Since the elephants are glass, many times the very act of wearing them caused trunks and legs to break off. An elephant bracelet in perfect condition might sell for as much as $250.00. The bracelets came in several different designs, with pink or green elephants, with four, six or eight elephants, and a mix of beads and pearls.

The bracelet that looks like fruit has sold at auction recently for as little as $60.00 to as much as almost $400.00. Condition brings higher prices for this design too, because it is often found with one or both of the tiny cherry beads missing.

The Asian designs feature buddhas, coins, fake jade, and beads, among other Asian-theme charms. The Egyptian-theme bracelets have scarabs and elaborate silver and glass charms. The bobbles bracelets have colored Lucite beads hanging below bead caps in different sizes and a variety of colors. Some feature all pink, all purple, or all blue beads, while others may have pink and blue beads and still others have pink and blue and purple and green beads. These bracelets all appeal to collectors. Nearly every time I search for Napier bracelets I can find another design I haven't yet seen. These bracelets are all very popular right now and command prices from $50.00 to close to $200.00.

Some of the bracelets, such as the Lucite bobbles, are made of plastic, while others are glass. The beaded designs come in pastels and in primary colors. And the bracelets that hold the charms also came in a wide variety. Some were multi-links together, while others are single wide or single narrow links. Many designs came in both gold tone and silver tone. One fabulous little design has four white glass bead heads of men and women; the men wear different types of hats while the women have different hair.

All of these Napier designs fall into the "fun" category for collectors. And they look great when worn two or more at a time. Many dealers are unaware of the popularity of these designs and it is possible to find them for as little as $20.00. You may get lucky and find the fruit charm bracelet for a small price, but if you decide you have to add one to your collection, be prepared to pay dearly for it. You will be wearing it for a long time, and perhaps passing it down to your grandchildren. After all, the bracelets with these timeless designs are already 40 or 50 years old.

This Napier charm style bracelet has light weight white barrel beads. It is 7½" long. **$65.00 – 75.00.** Author collection.

To add a charm bracelet to your collection, consider those found at Laurel Ladd Ciotti's site of vintage costume jewelry with charm bracelets found at www.eclecticala.com/charmed/charmed.htm.

This black beaded Napier charm style bracelet is 7" long and the clasp is marked. It looks great when worn with the matching white beaded Napier bracelet. And it makes a joyful noise. **$55.00 – 85.00.** Author collection.

This Napier bracelet has very large white plastic beads and is 7½" long. It is marked with a hang tag. Beads are over ½" in diameter. **$75.00 – 95.00.** Author collection.

Napier charm style bracelet with dangling gold-tone bead shapes. the textured bracelet is 7" long. **$125.00 – 150.00.** Author collection.

This Napier dangling leaves bracelet is 7" long and marked with a hang tag. **$65.00 – 85.00.** Author collection.

Totally gaudy set of Napier bracelet and earrings with fat pastel beads. All pieces are signed. The bracelet is 7½" and the earrings are 1⅝" wide. **$100.00 – 125.00.** Author collection.

This gold-tone Napier donkey charm bracelet also came in silver tone. The bracelet clasp is signed, as is the belly of the donkey. It is 7¾" long. **$55.00 – 75.00.** Author collection.

Napier silver-tone bell charm bracelet with crystal bead bell clapper. It also came in gold tone. The bracelet is signed and is 7¾". **$55.00 – 75.00.** Author collection.

This Napier bracelet has two charms attached but I don't know if either one is original. The locket opens to hold two photos and the watch is signed arpeggio. The bracelet is 7" long. **$75.00 – 95.00.** Author collection.

This Oriental style charm bracelet with glass jade charms looks like the Napier designs, but it is probably West German. It is unsigned, has eleven charms, and is 7¼". **$45.00 – 55.00.** Author collection.

This delightful charm style bracelet in red, white, and black, is signed "Les Bernard." It has loads of polka dotted and striped plastic beads on a black metal chain. The bracelet has a hang tag and is 7" long. **$45.00 – 65.00.** Author collection.

Charm style bracelet signed "Karla Jordan." The bracelet features glass and plastic bead charms. It is 7" long and is signed with a hang tag. **$25.00 – 45.00.** Author collection.

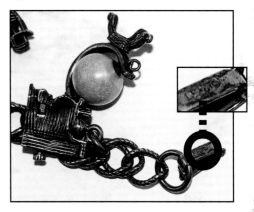

This Leru charm bracelet mimics a European trip souvenir with Oriental charms, an elephant, a train, hot air balloon, a globe, and an old time-y bicycle. **$95.00 – 125.00.** Author collection.

Leru mark on clasp.

This souvenir charm bracelet is marked "Made in France" and features architectural wonders. The bracelet is 7" long and the Eiffel tower charm is 1⅛" tall. **$100.00 – 125.00.** Author collection.

Made in France mark on clasp.

My search for this bracelet took me five years. As a cat lover in general, and a lover of Siamese cats in particular, I had to have this bracelet from the Disney movie That Darn Cat. Apparently it is a quite popular design. The bracelet is 6½" long and the two sitting cats are signed "Walt Disney Productions." **$25.00 – 35.00.** Author collection.

Quality

Collectors know quality the minute they see it. It is quite obvious from a distance. It is not necessary to pick up a piece of jewelry before deciding if it is quality. Nearly every designer made jewelry that falls into this category, but not all jewelry made by a designer will. Coro made jewelry that originally sold for pennies and some that sold for big money in exclusive boutiques. The high-end Coro jewelry will fall into the quality category, while most of the dime store pieces will not. This chapter shows you some jewelry that has been well made and that has stood the test of time, showing its quality.

Here is a real beauty by William de Lillo. This exquisite pin has red and green glass cabochons accented with clear stones and made in two pieces for movement. It is 5" x 3". The blue drops are glass. **$350.00 – 395.00.** Carol Bell Treasures-In-Time collection.

Day and evening grande parure by Mazer Bros. The heart-shaped glass stones have the look of poured glass and are accented by clear rhinestones. The set has three pins and two different sizes of earrings. All the pieces are signed. The necklace is 14½", the bracelet is 7", the large pin is 1¾" in diameter, the flower pin with stem and leaves is 2¼", the small pin is 1¼". The larger earrings are 1½" and the smaller earrings are 1⅛" in diameter. **$1,000.00 – 1,200.00.** Author collection.

Mazer Bros. heart glass bracelet with matching pin in bright yellow. The bracelet is 6¾" and the pin is 1¼" tall. **$200.00 – 225.00.** Author collection.

I recently discovered this set also came in baby blue. This pin is 1¾" in diameter. **$95.00 – 125.00.** Author collection.

Joseff Hollywood navy blue leaf in gold-tone setting, thermoset plastic is Tenite, 3½" x 2". **$325.00 – 350.00.** Carol Bell Treasures-In-Time collection.

Joseff necklace, 17". **$395.00 – 495.00.** Carol Bell Treasures-In-Time collection.

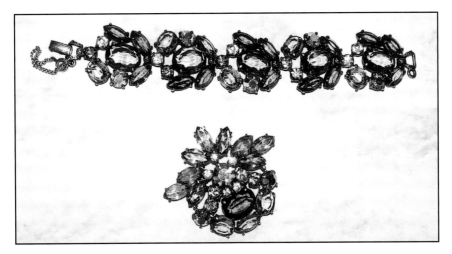

This Schiaparelli set has dark green, amber, blue, and clear rhinestones with a striking use of large stones. The larger more colorful stones are unfoiled and open backed. The bracelet is 7½" x 1¼" and the pin is 2" x 2½". **$850.00 – 950.00 for the set.** Carol Bell Treasures-In-Time collection.

This Joseff Hollywood necklace features topaz rhinestones with scrolls around the large center stone, 20" long. **$375.00 – 400.00.** Carol Bell Treasures-In-Time collection.

Stunning Joseff gilt necklace with dark blue and clear rhinestones. The blue rhinestones are unfoiled, the clear are gold foiled, the necklace is 15" long with the center design measuring 3½". **$875.00 – 900.00.** Carol Bell Treasures-In-Time collection.

This incredible bracelet was purchased from the estate of actress Ann Miller and is attributed to Kenneth Jay Lane. The centerpiece of an enormous ruby red cabochon is surrounded by clear rhinestones. The bracelet also features green glass cabochons around the sides and back, and is hinged. **$895.00 – 995.00.** Carol Bell Treasures-In-Time collection.

Joseff pin with gilt leaves and topaz rhinestones, 2¾" x 2¾". **$240.00 – 265.00.** Carol Bell Treasures-In-Time collection.

Your key to Hollywood! This Joseff key pin has a very large ruby red rhinestone. **$150.00 – 165.00.** Carol Bell Treasures-In-Time collection.

Joseff leaf pin and earring set. The pin has red rhinestones but the matching earrings have none. The pin is 3" x 3" and the earrings are 1¾" x 1¼", and only the pin is signed. **$350.00 – 365.00.** Carol Bell Treasures-In-Time collection.

Joseff dress clip with amethyst cabochon rhinestones. 3" x 2". **$265.00 – 285.00.** Carol Bell Treasures-In-Time collection.

These Joseff Oriental motif earrings are 2¼" long with large red cabochon dangles and pink AB cabochons at the top. **$295.00 – 325.00.** Carol Bell Treasures-In-Time collection.

This Joseff gilt brass oak leaf and acorn necklace, like most of the Joseff jewelry featured in this book, is from the 1940s. The pendant can be removed and worn as a pin. The necklace is 19" long with the pin/pendant measuring 3¼" tall. **$900.00 – 950.00.** Carol Bell Treasures-In-Time collection.

Reverse view of acorn necklace.

Joseff gilt brass Buddha necklace. Buddha is hanging on the front of the pendant. **$400.00 – 425.00.** Carol Bell Treasures-In-Time collection.

Joseff Russian gold bird pin with red and clear rhinestones, 2¾" x 2½". **$550.00 – 575.00.** Carol Bell Treasures-In-Time collection.

Joseff Russian gold pin with clear and amber rhinestones, 2¼" x 2¼". **$225.00 – 250.00.** Carol Bell Treasures-In-Time collection.

Joseff Russian gold pin with dangling clear crystals, 3½" long. **$250.00 – 275.00.** Carol Bell Treasures-In-Time collection.

Joseff elaborate fleur de lis earrings with clear and amethyst rhinestones, and scroll and pierced work. 4½" tall and nearly 2" wide. **$300.00 – 325.00.** Carol Bell Treasures-In-Time collection.

This Joseff ruby red rhinestone gilt brass bracelet is from the 1930s. It has a push-in clasp and is 8" long and 1" wide. **$475.00 – 500.00.** Carol Bell Treasures-In-Time collection.

Reverse view of bracelet showing Joseff Hollywood square plaque.

One of my personal favorite Stanley Hagler N.Y.C pins with green glass grapes, a green glass leaf, and amethyst rhinestones. No photograph can capture the beauty of this pin. **$350.00 – 375.00.** Carol Bell Treasures-In-Time collection.

Stanley Hagler bar pin in black and gold. The beads are hand wired on the gilt filigree setting, 3⅜" x 1". **$135.00 – 155.00.** Carol Bell Treasures-In-Time collection.

Wonderfully feminine Stanley Hagler N.Y.C. faux pearl earrings. These shoulder duster earrings are 4½" tall. **$275.00 – 300.00.** Carol Bell Treasures-In-Time collection.

Reverse view showing signature plate.

Stanley Hagler blues pin with glass beads. 2½" x 3". **$195.00 – 225.00.** Carol Bell Treasures-In-Time collection.

Miriam Haskell parure of turquoise colored glass necklace, bracelet and earrings, with glass beads and gilt petals. The necklace is 15" long, the bracelet is 8" long, and the earrings are 1¼" x 1". **$1,400.00 – 1,600.00.** Sheila Wukitsch collection.

Close-up view of necklace.

Close-up view of bracelet.

Close-up view of earrings.

Hollycraft 1954 set of bracelet, and pin. The bracelet is 8" long and the pin is 2½" x 2". **$500.00 – 800.00.** Sheila Wukitsch collection.

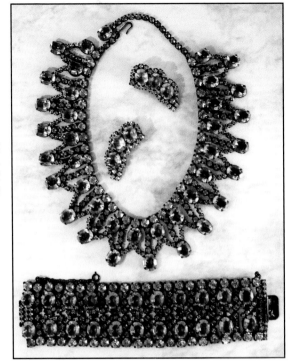

Hobé parure of necklace, bracelet, and earrings in japanned setting with aqua and clear rhinestones. The necklace is 16" long and 1½" wide, the bracelet is 7" x 1¾", and the earrings are 1½" x ⅝". $1,250.00 – 1,450.00. Sheila Wukitsch collection.

Miriam Haskell parure of topaz glass includes necklace, earrings, and pin. The necklace is 16" long, the pin is 3" x 2½", and the earrings are 1¼" diameter. $1,500.00 – 1,800.00. Sheila Wukitsch collection.

Reverse view of pin with signature plaque.

This gilt filigree pin and earrings set is by William de Lillo. The center of the pin, and the dangles of the earrings, have mirrors mounted in them for a unique design. The pin is 3" x 2½" with rose montees. The earrings have butterfly tops and are 3" long. Only the earrings are signed. $200.00 – 225.00. Carol Bell Treasures-In-Time collection.

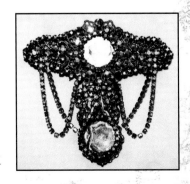

View of pin by itself.

Gorgeous William de Lillo ruby pendant with clear rhinestones. Note the clasp is a pierce work butterfly. The necklace is signed in two places and is 23" long. The pendant is 3" x 2¾". **$650.00 – 725.00.** Carol Bell Treasures-In-Time collection.

This tassel necklace is by William de Lillo and has faux pearls and red, blue, and green glass beads. It is 20" long with a 4" tassel. **$350.00 – 395.00.** Carol Bell Treasures-In-Time collection.

This Schiaparelli bracelet and earrings set has kite-shaped stones in topaz and citrine. The bracelet is 8" x 2" and the earrings are 1½" x 1". **$800.00 – 900.00.** Treasures-In-Time collection.

This Ciner collar necklace has green glass cabochons with clear pavé rhinestones. The necklace is 15½" long with a push-in clasp. **$900.00 – 1,100.00.** Carol Bell Treasures-In-Time collection.

Side view of necklace showing links.

Vogue Sterling green rhinestone pin with clear accents and two red stone eyes. It is 3¼". **$350.00 – 375.00.** Carol Bell Treasures-In-Time collection.

Joseff shoulder duster earrings with ivory-like dangling circles, 4" long. **$225.00 – 255.00.** Carol Bell Treasures-In-Time collection.

Joseff Hollywood bracelet with red stones, is 7¾" long. **$600.00 – 700.00.** Carol Bell Treasures-In-Time collection.

These Russian gold finish Joseff Hollywood tassel earrings dangle 3½". **$185.00 – 225.00.** Carol Bell Treasures-In-Time collection.

These Scaasi chandelier earrings have large red glass stones accented with clear rhinestones. The earrings are 2⅞" and are signed. Scaasi is Isaacs spelled backwards, for the designer's name — Arnold Isaacs. **$275.00 – 300.00.** Carol Bell Treasures-In-Time collection.

Here is a really bold cuff bracelet design in dark and light pink, signed "Sorrel Originals." **$600.00 – 650.00.** Carol Bell Treasures-In-Time collection.

Incredibly beautiful Christian Dior necklace with clear and pale yellow rhinestone tear and marquise stones in a leafy flower design. It is 18" long and is signed. **$600.00 – 700.00.** Carol Bell Treasures-In-Time collection.

Quality

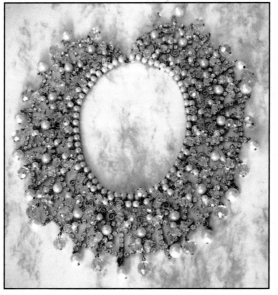

This substantial collar necklace was made by KJL and features faux pearls, rhinestones, and crystal beads. **$2,200.00 – 2,400.00.** Carol Bell Treasures-In-Time collection.

CIS snowball or dandelion pin with pink, green, and lavender prong-set rhinestones. This is the most well known CIS design, 2½" in diameter. **$450.00 – 550.00.** Carol Bell Treasures-In-Time collection.

Reverse view of CIS pin, note trombone closure on pin stem.

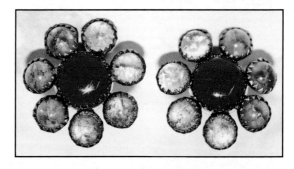

Close-up of CIS earrings.

CIS necklace and earrings set in luscious pink, rose, and green cabochons and rhinestones. The necklace is 18½" long and the earrings are 1½". **$2,000.00 – 2,300.00.** Carol Bell Treasures-In-Time collection.

Reverse view of earring showing stamped signature which includes a crown at the top.

78

This lovely French necklace features gorgeous oversize topaz emerald-cut rhinestones accented with clear and amber rhinestones. The choker necklace is 16½" long. **$350.00 – 450.00.** Treasures-In-Time collection.

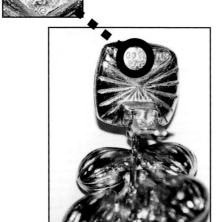

These rare Robert Goossens earrings in autumn colors dangle 3" and feature glass cabochons. They are signed "Goossens Paris." Earrings are articulated for wonderful movement and are 1¼" wide. **$345.00 – 375.00.** Treasures-In-Time collection.

Reverse view of earrings showing Goossens Paris signature.

This Tortolani jester pin with black and clear rhinestones is a whopping 4⅞" x 2" and it is made in two parts so the post swings freely. **$325.00 – 350.00.** Barbara Wood collection.

This beautiful flower pin has green poured glass petals and is accented with green and clear rhinestones. It is signed "Barclay" and measures 2¼" x 1½". **$149.00 – 179.00.** Barbara Wood collection.

Reverse view showing signature.

Coro Craft Sterling jelly belly pin with huge Lucite belly. The fish is accented with clear rhinestones and a red stone eye. The center stone is nearly 1½" wide. The pin is 2½" x 2½". **$450.00 – 550.00.** Elizabeth Cooper collection.

Close up view of signature mark.

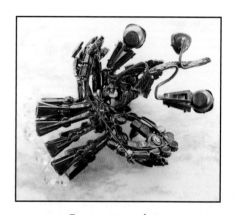

This astonishing brooch is a one-of-a-kind masterpiece by Larry Vrba and is a colossal 6". This magnificent piece features black AB marquise stones, a variety of black glass stones, and large and medium clear rhinestones topped by clear crystals. This piece is very heavy, and is handmade, and signed with the Lawrence Vrba plaque. It is nearly 4" wide. A true work of art. **$595.00 – 695.00.** Barbara Wood collection.

Top view showing crystals.

Reverse view of pin.

This extraordinary brooch with matching earrings features a centerpiece depicting Lucretia Borgia, who was reputed to be the most evil woman who ever lived. This original set by Lawrence Vrba honors her with a circlet of large amethyst glass stones, unfoiled and open backed, accented with clear rhinestones. The gold-tone centerpiece is actually signed "Italy" on the back. The brooch is 4" in diameter and the earrings are 1½". **$450.00 – 550.00 for the set.** Barbara Wood collection.

This Weinberg pin is an example of costume jewelry mimicking fine jewelry. It has clear rhinestones and lapis colored cabochons. The pin is signed "Weinberg New York" and is 3¼" x 2". Weinberg is a rare name to find. **$145.00 – 165.00.** Barbara Wood collection.

Reverse view of pin.

Another stunning design by Larry Vrba features a Greek god surrounded by blue tear-drop glass stones and clear rhinestones. Large blue stones are unfoiled and open backed. The set includes matching earrings. The brooch is over 4" in diameter and the earrings are 1½", and all three pieces are signed. **$625.00 – 725.00.** Barbara Wood collection.

This unsigned Miriam Haskell stickpin is ultra feminine with tiny hand-wired pearls accented with rhinestones. The top design on the stick pin is 2", while the overall length including dangles is 4". **$250.00 – 300.00.** Barbara Wood collection.

The unsigned Miriam Haskell stick pin features a design of a flower over a wreath. The top part of the design measures 2½" while the overall length including dangles is 5". **$250.00 – 300.00.** Barbara Wood collection.

These exquisite earrings show the design genius of the man who was once the head designer for Miriam Haskell. These earrings have baroque pearls in shades of gray and clear rhinestones wired together. As with all of the Larry Vrba designs, these are handmade. The earrings are 2¼" in diameter. **$75.00 – 100.00.** Barbara Wood collection.

Chanel dangle earrings with a red glass teardrop below a green glass teardrop inside a clear glass ring and below a black glass square. These unusual beauties are 4" long and are signed "Chanel" on the back of the ear clip. They are priced with their original box. **$425.00 – 450.00**. Carol Bell Treasures-In-Time collection.

Reverse view of earring showing signature.

This Chanel faux pearl and rhinestone choker from the 1980s is signed on the back of a pearl next to the clasp. This necklace features large clear rhinestones as beads. **$625.00 – 650.00.** Carol Bell Treasures-In-Time collection.

View of necklace showing signature.

Chanel green poured glass pin/pendant cross in gold-plated setting. The huge pin is 5" tall and 2⅞" wide. It is signed on the back "Chanel, Made in France" and "94P." **$545.00 – 575.00.** Carol Bell Treasures-In-Time collection.

This Chanel fur clip is from the 1980s and is probably a Gripoix design. It has a faux pearl dangling below two large rhinestones, which are surrounded by amethyst poured glass. This beautiful and totally feminine clip is 4½" long and the two rhinestone disks measure 1¼" in diameter, with the pearl drop being ¾". **$525.00 – 550.00.** Carol Bell Treasures-In-Time collection.

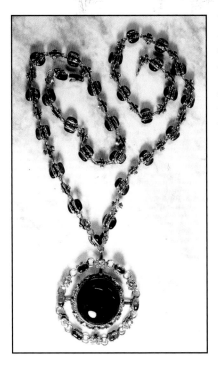

This more contemporary Chanel neck-lace from the 1995 season features an amethyst cabochon in a pendant measuring 2¼" in diameter. Look closely at the chain which has amethyst cabochons as links. It is 30" long. **$995.00 – 1,050.00.** Carol Bell Treasures-In-Time collection.

This glorious bracelet features caged Lucite balls in two different sizes. It measures almost 10" but because of the size of it, it is not too big around a normal size wrist. There is a hang tag at the clasp that says "Monette of Paris" on one side and "Made in France" on the other. Another piece of joyful noise jewelry. **$200.00 – 225.00.** Author collection.

This exquisite pin is made of green glass and clear rhinestones, and mimics fine jewelry. It is 3½" x 1¾". **$225.00 – 250.00.** Carol Bell Treasures-In-Time collection.

View showing B.B. mark.

This rhinestone bracelet is marked "B.B.," the mark of the E.A. Bennet company which began in business in 1892 in Providence, Rhode Island. The bracelet with safety chain is 7" long. The clasp becomes hidden when fastened. A rare find. **$350.00 – 400.00.** Author collection.

This amazing necklace by Weinberg of New York looks like a copy of royal jewels. The pendant has a watermelon stone and each link has either an amethyst colored cabochon or three unfaceted marquis stones. Each link is outlined with clear rhinestones and the amethyst stones are unfoiled and open backed. It is 16" long. **$295.00 – 345.00.** Barbara Wood collection.

Here is a rare and unusual set of Les Bernard jewelry from the Dynasty TV Series Collection. Each piece has its own pouch and snaps hold the jewelry in position. None of the pieces are signed. The large clear beads are all crystal. The heavy necklace with the snowflake rhinestone balls is 16" long. The pierced earrings are over 2" long. **$200.00 – 250.00.** Author collection.

Necklace inside pouch.

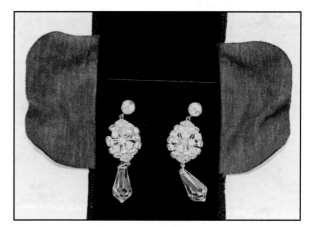

Earrings inside pouch.

Brania rhinestone pin with green accents. The round green stones are bezel set on wire giving this pin beautiful movement. **$225.00 – 250.00.** Carol Bell Treasures-In-Time collection.

Reverse view of pin with signature plaque.

I love the design on these EDLEE clip-on earrings. The large glass stones are a purple that fades to blue. The earrings are both signed and are 1½" tall. **$45.00 – 65.00.** Author collection.

Artful Plastics

The market is still being flooded with fake Bakelite, and newly made plastic jewelry called French Bakelite, but that hasn't affected the prices collectors are willing to pay for the good stuff. Fruit jewelry, the better designs, and the best genuine bracelets still bring high prices.

Novice collectors need to educate themselves before beginning a Bakelite collection, in order to protect themselves and their investment.

Bakelite palm tree with three coconuts dangling at the top. The tree has a brad attaching the fronds to the trunk to allow it to sway, the pin back is embedded in the front. It is 3½" tall. **$400.00 – 475.00.** Author collection.

Reverse view of tree pin.

Brania gold-tone pin with large green centerpiece made of Bakelite and accented with clear and blue rhinestones. The pin is 3½" by 3¼" with the Bakelite center measuring 1¾" in diameter. **$245.00 – 265.00.** Carol Bell Treasures-In-Time collection.

This Bakelite carved red dress clip is 2⅜" x ⅞". **$65.00 – 75.00.** Author collection.

This Bakelite turtle in ice tea and apple juice is made of two pieces of Bakelite with tiny screws as eyes. 1⅞" x 1⅛". **$95.00 – 125.00.** Author collection.

Bakelite green Prystal carved dress clip with an attached gold-tone band. 2¼" x 1¼". **$50.00 – 75.00.** Author collection.

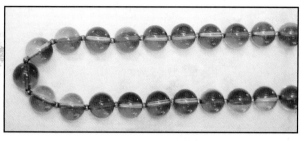

Fabulous set of two tone Lucite beads in green and blue. This push-in clasp features half of a bead. The necklace is 27" long. Notice the Napier vanity girl jewelry holder on the back cover is holding this necklace. **$65.00 – 95.00.** Author collection.

Bakelite carved green banana pin with a brown top. 2½" long. **$125.00 – 150.00.** Author collection.

This carved red Bakelite bar pin is 2¾" wide. **$95.00 – 125.00.** Author collection.

This faceted Bakelite oval red pin is 2⅜" wide. **$100.00 – 140.00.** Author collection.

This Prystal red Bakelite dress clip is carved front and back and is 2³⁄₁₆". **$135.00 – 160.00.** Author collection.

Another carved Prystal red Bakelite dress clip, 1⅝" tall. **$125.00 – 150.00.** Author collection.

Reverse view of Prystal dress clips.

Here is a pair of carved grapes pins with apple juice and dark brown Bakelite. This is one of my favorite sets, since it was a Valentine's gift from my husband. **$175.00 – 200.00.** Author collection.

Reverse view of Bakelite pin.

My very favorite Bakelite earrings are this pair of crowing roosters in dark green Bakelite with red painted eyes. The earrings are screw on and measure 1¼" tall. These are very rare. **$175.00 – 200.00.** Author collection.

A triple dose of Prystal. These Bakelite dress clips look like blueberry juice, lime juice, and cherry juice. The clips are 1¾" x 1⅛". Each clip is worth **$95.00 – 125.00,** as a matched set the price would be **$375.00 – 450.00.** Author collection.

Pear-shaped Bakelite dress clips in avocado green. 1⅞" tall. **$95.00 – 120.00.** Author collection.

This striking celluloid flower scarf clip has such beautiful rhinestones that I don't know what color to call them. Maybe bright light emerald green. The clip measures almost 2". **$55.00 – 75.00.** Author collection.

This red Bakelite resting cat pin is 3" long. **$125.00 – 150.00.** Author collection.

This orange carved Bakelite flower dress clip has been given a pearlized coating. 2¼" x 1⅝". **$75.00 – 95.00.** Author collection.

This caramel Bakelite carved dress clip is 1⅝" x 1⅛". **$65.00 – 75.00.** Author collection.

I believe as more and more new Bakelite artists and crafts people take apart Bakelite beaded necklaces to use for parts, the prices will rise slightly. This creamy apricot necklace with graduated beads is 22" long. **$95.00 – 110.00.** Author collection.

This necklace with caramel Bakelite oval graduated beads has a large center bead in an orange juice color. The end beads make the screw-on barrel clasp. It is 24½". **$125.00 – 150.00.** Author collection.

This deep dark Bakelite cherry juice graduated oval bead necklace is 28" long and fits over your head. **$150.00 – 175.00.** Author collection.

This Bakelite bright cherry juice round bead necklace with built-in barrel clasp is 30" long. **$175.00 – 200.00.** Author collection.

Bakelite orange button earrings, 1" in diameter. **$25.00 – 45.00.** Author collection.

Orange Bakelite seems to be more affordable than other colors, I guess because few collectors are interested in orange. This great beaded necklace is 26" long. **$100.00 – 125.00.** Author collection.

This orange Bakelite expandable link bracelet has links that are 1½" x ⅞". Expandable bracelets are great for those who can't wear the Bakelite bangles. **$125.00 – 150.00.** Author collection.

Carved Bakelite button earrings in transparent green with swirls of green, ⅞" in diameter. **$55.00 – 65.00.** Author collection.

This Bakelite bracelet was made with butterscotch tube beads and creamed spinach green beads on elastic. **$95.00 – 125.00.** Author collection.

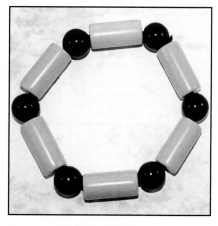

Matching Bakelite bracelet with brown beads. **$95.00 – 125.00.** Author collection.

This wonderful Bakelite necklace with graduated oval beads has an amazing color which looks like dark cherry juice swirled with orange juice. The necklace is strung on chain and is 30" long with largest beads being ¾" wide. **$175.00 – 200.00.** Author collection.

This Bakelite necklace has cherry vanilla beads mounted on memory wire. It is 15" long. **$150.00 – 175.00.** Author collection.

Shultz Bakelite parrot head pin in cherry red, black, and lemon lime Bakelite with a glass eye. The pin is signed and is 3" x 2¾". **$500.00 – 550.00.** Author collection.

This bracelet is made using Bakelite mah jong tiles. The best of these designs use all Bakelite beads and the older, more elaborate designed tiles are more valuable. These bracelets are extremely popular. This one has quite thick tiles, and creamed spinach Bakelite beads. These bracelets are also reversible, if you want to wear the plain side of the tiles. This one was a gift from my husband and I will always treasure it. Mah jong bracelets are valued between **$20.00** and **$100.00**, depending on tiles and beads. Author collection.

Lucite earrings with a bluebird inside each one. The earrings have screw-on backs and measure ¾" in diameter. **$35.00 – 50.00.** Author collection.

This pair of Lucite sweater guards has genuine miniature seahorses embedded inside. The clasp of each guard is signed "Pat. Pending." The Lucite measures ¾" x ¾". **$45.00 – 55.00.** Author collection.

This celluloid necklace has little bubbles with removable tops to allow you to insert whatever you like that will fit. These hold tiny green feathers. It is quite a fun little piece. It is 14½" long and currently missing its clasp, but I have just the right one to use as a replacement. **$95.00 – 125.00.** Author collection.

Close-up view of bubbles, the caps pop off like Christmas ornament tops.

This unsigned penguin pair have bodies like carved jelly bellies with one slender penguin and one fat penguin. The large penguin is 2¾", the small penguin is 2¼", and the chain joining the two is 5" long. **$150.00 – 195.00.** Author collection.

Jim Foltz is a Bakelite artist with a humorous design ethic. His work brings a quick smile to the face of any collector. Scottie pins have always been Bakelite collector favorites and here Foltz renders his Scottie driving a convertible and wearing a gold scarf. The back is signed "J. L. Foltz '04." It is 1⅜" x 1". **$75.00 – 95.00.** Author collection.

This little political donkey pin with teeth is a Foltz original. The pin is signed "J. L. Foltz '04" and is 1⅜" x 1¼". **$50.00 – 75.00.** Author collection.

This Foltz Bakelite flamingo pin casts a shy eye at viewers. It is signed "J. L. Foltz '03" and is 3⅛" tall. **$125.00 – 175.00.** Author collection.

This Foltz Bakelite necklace is a rare find, since Jim Foltz designs mainly pins. This necklace with a fishy theme has seven different fish with google eyes and red lips, when they have lips, that is. The fish on the right side is blue moon Bakelite. **$250.00 – 300.00.** Author collection.

Shultz white bracelet with blue dots, ½". **$325.00 – 350.00.** Barbara Wood collection.

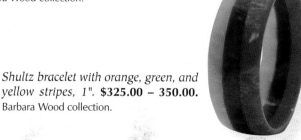

Shultz bracelet with orange, green, and yellow stripes, 1". **$325.00 – 350.00.** Barbara Wood collection.

Shultz butterscotch bracelet with lavender squares, 1". **$650.00 – 700.00.** Barbara Wood collection.

Shultz black bracelet with cherry and pink squares, 1". **$550.00 – 600.00.** Barbara Wood collection.

Shultz blue and white bracelet with apple juice and lavender, 1¾". **$695.00 – 745.00.** Barbara Wood collection.

Shultz black bracelet with green and lavender, 1⅛". **$550.00 – 600.00.** Barbara Wood collection.

Shultz bracelet with pale orange, yellow, and green stripes, 1". **$325.00 – 350.00.** Barbara Wood collection.

Shultz pink bracelet with black dots, ⅝". **$350.00 – 375.00.** Barbara Wood collection.

Shultz bracelet with yellow and green stripes, ½". **$250.00 – 275.00.** Barbara Wood collection.

Shultz blue bracelet with yellow, green, and pink colored inserts, ¾". **$395.00 – 425.00.** Barbara Wood collection.

Shultz green bracelet with white inserts, 1⁷⁄₁₆". **$500.00 – 550.00.** Barbara Wood collection.

Shultz checkerboard bracelet with yellow, green, purple, and orange, 1⅜". **$675.00 – 750.00.** Barbara Wood collection.

Shultz red multicolored bracelet with dovetail inserts, ⅞". **$550.00 – 600.00.** Barbara Wood collection.

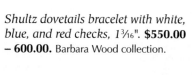

Shultz dovetails bracelet with white, blue, and red checks, 1³⁄₁₆". **$550.00 – 600.00.** Barbara Wood collection.

Shultz granite bracelet with yellow, red, blue, and black inserts, 1". **$525.00 – 575.00.** Barbara Wood collection.

Shultz red and white checkerboard bracelet, ⅞". **$675.00 – 750.00.** Barbara Wood collection.

Shultz multicolored checkerboard bracelet, 1⅛". **$725.00 – 775.00.** Barbara Wood collection.

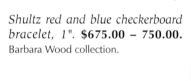

Shultz red and blue checkerboard bracelet, 1". **$675.00 – 750.00.** Barbara Wood collection.

Shultz apple juice bracelet with multicolored inserts, ⅞". **$550.00 – 650.00.** Barbara Wood collection.

Shultz checkerboard bracelet with lime juice and white, 1½". **$950.00 – 1,050.00.** Barbara Wood collection.

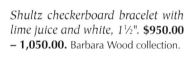

Shultz checkerboard bracelet with red, white, blue, yellow, and orange, 1½". **$950.00 – 1,050.00.** Barbara Wood collection.

Shultz one-of-a-kind colored and shaped checkerboard bracelet, 1¾" wide and over ½" thick. **$900.00 – 1,100.00.** Barbara Wood collection.

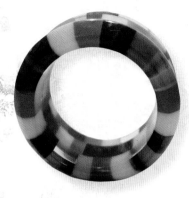

Shultz checkerboard bracelet with clear, black, red, and green, 1¼". **$800.00 – 875.00.** Barbara Wood collection.

Shultz checkerboard bracelet with green, yellow, blue, white, and red, 1". **$675.00 – 750.00.** Barbara Wood collection.

Shultz black and red bracelet with yellow, blue, and white squares, 1⅛". **$550.00 – 625.00.** Barbara Wood collection.

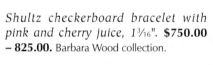

Shultz checkerboard bracelet with pink and cherry juice, 1³⁄₁₆". **$750.00 – 825.00.** Barbara Wood collection.

Shultz checkerboard bracelet with yellow, red, green, lavender, pink, and blue, 1³⁄₁₆". **$695.00 – 750.00.** Barbara Wood collection.

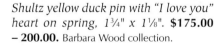

Shultz yellow duck pin with "I love you" heart on spring, 1¾" x 1⅛". **$175.00 – 200.00.** Barbara Wood collection.

Shultz Scottie dog pin with heart on spring, 1¾" x 1¾". **$175.00 – 200.00.** Barbara Wood collection.

Parures and Demi-Parures

Schiaparelli at her bluest in this set of pin and earrings with lava rock rhinestones in a gunmetal setting. All pieces are signed. The pin is 2¼" x 2" and the earrings are 1½" x ¾". **$495.00 – 525.00.** Carol Bell Treasures-In-Time collection.

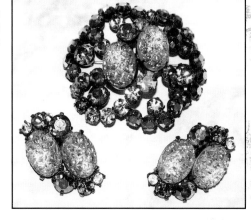

This fabulous Miriam Haskell set is a departure from her pearl designs. This set has pale blue crystal beads. The necklace is 32" long and has the Miriam Haskell hang tag. The two strand bracelet with the safety chain is 7" long. A rare set. **$250.00 – 300.00.** Author collection.

Schreiner New York strawberry set with earrings and two different pins. Only the small pin is signed. The larger pin is 2" x 1½", the smaller pin is 1" x 1½", and the earrings are ⅞" diameter. **$295.00 – 325.00.** Carol Bell Treasures-In-Time collection.

Impressive Schreiner New York pin and earrings with large bronze rhinestones surrounded by smoky silver rhinestones. The pin is 2¼" x 2" and the earrings are 1" x ⅞". **$340.00 – 365.00.** Carol Bell Treasures-In-Time collection.

Schreiner clear rhinestones pin and earrings with foil back stones in a gunmetal setting, highlighting the look of the clear stones. The pin is 2⅛" x 2" and the earrings are 1¼" x 1⅛". **$325.00 – 350.00.** Carol Bell Treasures-In-Time collection.

Beautiful Schreiner New York bracelet, pin, and earrings in shades of yellow with green and amber rhinestones. Only the bracelet is signed. The bracelet is 8" x 1½" with a push-in clasp and safety chain, the pin is 2⅛" x 2", and the earrings are 1¼" x 1⅛". Bracelet **$425.00 – 450.00** and unsigned pin and earrings **$300.00 – 325.00.** Carol Bell Treasures-In-Time collection.

Close-up view of pin and earrings.

Striking unsigned Schreiner pin and earrings with dark green cabochon stones outlined in pink and aqua rhinestones. The pin is 2" x 1½" and the earrings are 1½" x 1". **$325.00 – 350.00.** Carol Bell Treasures-In-Time collection.

Original by Robert red and pink pin and earrings in a gunmetal setting. The pin is signed "Original by Robert" and the earring are signed "Robert" in script. The pin is 2½" x 2" and the earrings are 1⅝" x 1". **$375.00 – 395.00.** Carol Bell Treasures-In-Time collection.

This Miriam Haskell set of pin and earrings features faceted black glass stones which are accented with petite rhinestone flowers. The pin is 2" in diameter and the earrings are 1⅛" x ⅞". The pin is signed in raised letters on an oval plaque and the earrings are signed on a horseshoe-shaped plaque. **$275.00 – 325.00.** Carol Bell Treasures-In-Time collection.

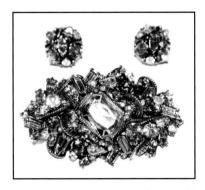

Stunning Eugene necklace and earrings in emerald green. The necklace has three strands of green glass beads separated by tiny gold beads. The lovely centerpiece has beads wired onto a gilt curved finding, which the earrings match. The necklace is 20" long and the earrings are 1½" long. All pieces are signed. **$345.00 – 375.00.** Carol Bell Treasures-In-Time collection.

This pin is instantly recognized as Hollycraft with the use of pastel rhinestones. It is marked "Hollycraft" and each piece is dated. The pin is 3" x 1¾" and is dated 1957 and the earrings are ⅝" diameter and dated 1953. **$275.00 – 300.00.** Carol Bell Treasures-In-Time collection.

Kramer red and blue pin and earrings set. All pieces are signed. **$245.00 – 265.00.** Carol Bell Treasures-In-Time collection.

Claudette ruby red teardrop set with square ruby red glass stones in a black japanned setting. Pin is 3" x 1⅜" and earrings are 1⅛" x 1". **$225.00 – 250.00.** Carol Bell Treasures-In-Time collection.

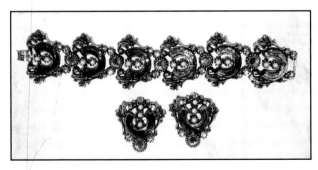

This wonderfully feminine Pome bracelet and earrings feature topaz and amber rhinestones accented with small faux pearls. Each link of the bracelet is signed, and both earrings are signed. The bracelet measures 7¼" x 1¼" and the earrings are 1¼" diameter. **$175.00 – 195.00.** Carol Bell Treasures-In-Time collection.

Reverse view of bracelet showing signature.

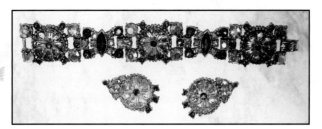

This Pome bracelet and earrings set with topaz and amber rhinestones is accented with clear rhinestones. All of the bracelet links are signed on the back. The bracelet is 7¼" x 1" and the earrings are 1½" x 1". **$195.00 – 225.00.** Carol Bell Treasures-In-Time collection.

This Trifari set of pin and earrings features baby teeth faux pearls in a gold-tone setting with clear stone accents. The set was made in the 1950s. Each piece has the Crown Trifari mark on it. The pin is 2½" x 1⅞" and the earrings are 1" in diameter. **$125.00 – 150.00.** Barbara Wood collection.

This ART set of pin and earrings is the sort that goes with just about everything in your closet. It has many different colors of stones, all faceted, and some with an AB finish. The pin and one earring are signed. The pin is 1⅞" in diameter and the earrings are 1⅛" tall. **$110.00 – 135.00.** Barbara Wood collection.

This Lisner parure appears to be Hollycraft at first glance, with its use of pale pastel rhinestones in a antiqued gold-tone setting. It is filled with pale yellow, pink, lavender, and green rhinestones. The necklace is 15½" long, the bracelet is 7" x ⅞", the earrings are 1¼" in diameter, and the pin is 2¼" x 1½". **$225.00 – 250.00.** Carol Bell Treasures-In-Time collection.

Kramer headlight set with dangle drop rhinestone necklace with clear stones in a gold-tone setting, bracelets, and earrings. Headlight sets are quite beautiful in person, big and bold. This necklace is signed "Kramer" and is 17" long. **$475.00 – 550.00.** Carol Bell Treasures-In-Time collection.

Here are the two matching headlight bracelets that go with the previous necklace. One bracelet is 7", the other is 7½".

This Original by Robert set of pin and earrings looks like a stylized pineapple. The set has topaz rhinestones, some with AB finish. **$295.00 – 350.00.** Carol Bell Treasures-In-Time collection.

Green means go! This Kramer headlight set in gold-tone has green cabochon glass stones. The necklace is 16", the bracelet is 7", and the earrings are 1" long. **$275.00 – 350.00.** Carol Bell Treasures-In-Time collection.

Kramer headlight set with faceted blue glass stones in silver-tone setting. The necklace is 15½" and the earrings are ¾". **$275.00 – 350.00.** Carol Bell Treasures-In-Time collection.

This Schreiner japanned set with clear rhinestones is a real beauty in person. The pin is 3¼" x 2½" and is not signed, though clearly part of the set. The earrings are signed and are 1¾" x ¾". **$450.00 – 495.00.** Carol Bell Treasures-In-Time collection.

This great Kramer pin and earring set has red and clear baguette rhinestones in a swirl setting. The pin is 2" in diameter and the earrings are 1". **$175.00 – 225.00.** Carol Bell Treasures-In-Time collection.

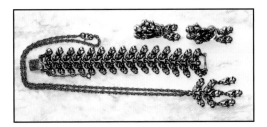

Here is a Tortolani necklace, bracelet, and earrings set in a flower bud design. **$150.00 – 175.00.** Carol Bell Treasures-In-Time collection.

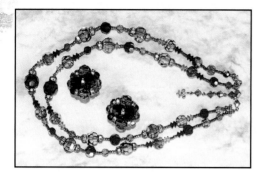

Vendôme did some wonderful colored bead jewelry and this set is bright and beautiful. It has hot pink and smoky crystal beads. The necklace is 17½" and the earrings are 1". **$125.00 – 165.00.** Carol Bell Treasures-In-Time collection.

This Pennino silver-tone leaf set has melon-shaped moonstone glass stones, each accented with a clear rhinestone. The bracelet and earrings are signed, but the necklace is not. The necklace is 16" long, the bracelet is 7" long, and the earrings are 1¼" x ¾". **$295.00 – 325.00.** Carol Bell Treasures-In-Time collection.

This Ornella set has a three-strand necklace with matching earrings with purple and green beads. The necklace is 16" and the earrings are 1". **$250.00 – 300.00.** Carol Bell Treasures-In-Time collection.

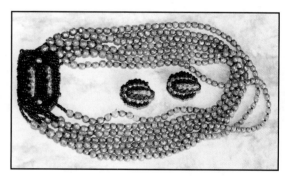

Another Ornella beaded set with faux pearls and turquoise, and bronze seed beads. The necklace is seven strands and is 16" long and the earrings are 1" long. **$350.00 – 400.00.** Carol Bell Treasures-In-Time collection.

Elegant Ciner necklace and bracelet set in gold-tone ribbed and overlapping links. **$400.00 – 475.00.** Carol Bell Treasures-In-Time collection.

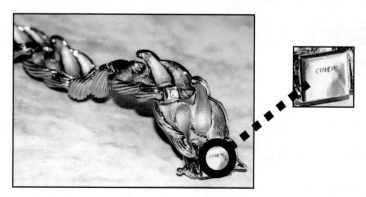

View of signature on Ciner necklace.

This beautiful Ciner set has red, green, and blue glass cabochons in a gold-tone setting. The necklace is 17" long and the bracelet is 7½". This set is from the 1980s. **$500.00 – 575.00.** Carol Bell Treasures-In-Time collection.

This Vogue set has amber AB crystal beads and rhinestone ball beads. The necklace is 14" long. **$375.00 – 395.00.** Carol Bell Treasures-In-Time collection.

This Miriam Haskell fringe bib necklace with matching bracelet set has toffee beads, faux pearls, and green and gold-tone beads. Both are signed. **$700.00 – 800.00.** Carol Bell Treasures-In-Time collection.

Here is an amazing set by Zoe Coste. Cher used to wear Zoe Coste when she was performing. This set is marked "Zoe Coste Made In Paris," all pieces are marked and one earring is marked twice. The set has flowers and a butterfly and amber and green glass stones, some of which are cabochons. **$350.00 – 425.00.** Carol Bell Treasures-In-Time collection.

Italian Ornella set of four strand necklace and earrings with white, pink, red, and green beads. The necklace is 17" long and the earrings are 1¼". **$550.00 – 600.00.** Carol Bell Treasures-In-Time collection.

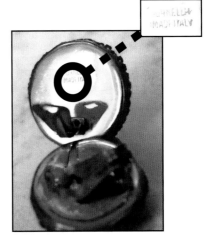

Reverse view of earring showing "Ornella Made Italy" stamped signature.

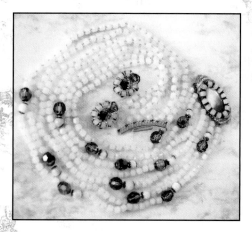

Ornella seven strand necklace with matching earrings of opal glass beads and AB crystal beads. The necklace is 17" long and the earrings are 1⅛". **$550.00 – 600.00.** Carol Bell Treasures-In-Time collection.

This Hobé set reminds me of speckled bird eggs. The clear art glass beads have blue speckles and the swirly white beads are plastic. Both ends of the necklace are signed as are both earrings. Beads are strung on a chain. The adjustable two-strand necklace is 16" long with an extension allowing 3½" and the earrings are 1" in diameter. **$125.00 – 150.00.** Author collection.

This Hobé pink glass set is extremely feminine. All of the beads are glass and they are strung on a chain. The necklace is 15" long with an extension allowing 3". The bracelet is mounted on memory wire to fit any size wrist. **$150.00 – 175.00.** Author collection.

Close-up view of bracelet.

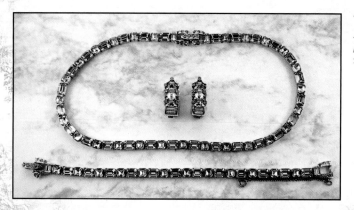

This stunning Mazer Bros. parure in pale lavender is a real find. Each piece is signed and they are in excellent condition. The necklace is 14½" long, the bracelet is 7½" long, and the earrings are ⅞". **$400.00 – 450.00.** Author collection.

Close-up view of earrings.

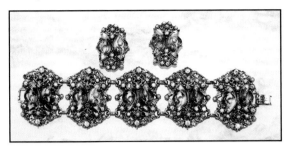

This unsigned set has a Florenza look to it. It is set with unusual pale blue glass stones, AB stones, and tiny faux pearls. The bracelet is 7½" long and the earrings are 1⅜" x 1". **$95.00 – 125.00.** Author collection.

Claudette set with blue glass cabochons and blue and clear rhinestones. I believe this was a bracelet that someone removed the clasp from so they could add the chain and turn it into a necklace, but I could be wrong, since the design does speak of being a necklace. The necklace is 17" long and the earrings are 1". Both earrings are signed. **$65.00 – 80.00.** Author collection.

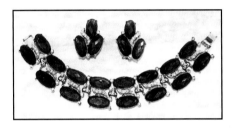

Claudette silver-tone flower necklace and earring set. The necklace is 13½" long and earrings are 1⅝" tall. Both earrings are marked. The clasp has been changed on this necklace, too. **$75.00 – 90.00.** Author collection.

Claudette silver-tone set with large flat blue glass oval stones and clear rhinestone accents. The bracelet is 7¼" long and the earrings are 1⅜", all three pieces are marked. **$75.00 – 95.00.** Author collection.

Claudette earrings on original card matching previous pin. The earrings are unmarked and are 1" in diameter. **$25.00 – 30.00.** Author collection.

This Claudette pin on its original card also has the original price tag marked "$1.00" and "Stix, Baer & Fuller," a former department store originally located in Missouri. The pin is 2¼" tall. **$45.00 – 60.00.** *Price for set* **$80.00 – 90.00.** Author collection.

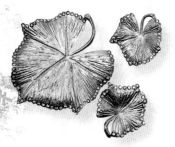

Claudette textured pin with matching earrings. Only the earrings are marked. The pin is 2¼" and the earrings are 1". These were a gift from a dear friend. **$75.00 – 95.00.** Author collection.

Shades of pink and green rhinestones make up this beautiful necklace with matching earrings. The necklace is unsigned and is 17", while the earrings are 1¹⁄₁₆". **$85.00 – 110.00.** Author collection.

This fun and unusual set is unsigned. The pin has an Asian man carrying a yoke with two large green art glass cabochons, and each earring is a hat with identical dangles. The pin is 2¼" x 2" and the earrings dangle 1¾". **$150.00 – 175.00.** Author collection.

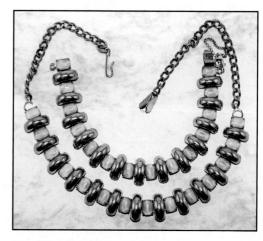

Capri japanned pink and lavender flower set. All pieces are signed but the signature is very difficult to see. The pin is 2⅜" tall and the earrings are 1⅛". **$65.00 – 85.00.** Author collection.

This blue moonstone demi parure is unsigned but well made. The necklace is 15" long and the bracelet is 6¾". **$150.00 – 175.00.** Author collection.

Here is an extremely rare set of Mazer Bros. jewelry with pink glass scarabs. The glass stones are even etched on the reverse side. Only the pin and earrings are signed. I believe the necklace was signed but the plating has worn off the clasp. The pin has the tiniest legible signature I have ever seen on a piece of jewelry. Without using magnification, it appears as a minuscule imperfection in the finish. The necklace is 15" long, the pin is 2" and the earrings are ¾". **$450.00 – 500.00.** Author collection.

Matching set of Claudette thermoplastic necklace and bracelet in aqua and lavender. The bracelet is signed. **$75.00 – 85.00.** Author collection.

This set in its original box is Star-Art Sterling and each piece is signed. All the clear rhinestones are prong set. The pin is 2" x 1¼" and the earrings are 1⅛". **$95.00 – 125.00.** Author collection.

Claudette stylized star pin with matching earrings in amethyst and blue rhinestones, and gunmetal finish. The pin is almost 3" in diameter and the earrings are 1⅜". Only the earrings are marked, as is standard with most Claudette jewelry. The rhinestones are glued in with the appearance of prongs. **$200.00 – 225.00.** Author collection.

After years of searching I finally scored a Claudette set with the necklace and bracelet. Claudette jewelry has been extremely hard for me to add to my collection since my first book came out, so I was thrilled to find this set. This glorious set in a gunmetal finish has greens, blues, and AB rhinestones. The earrings are identical to the set pictured below with the pinwheel design, look at the center of the pin to see the earring. Only the earrings are marked but it is clearly a set. The necklace is 16¾" long, the bracelet is 7½" long, and the earrings are over 1" in diameter. **$650.00 – 750.00.** Author collection.

Colorful Claudette set of stylized star pin and earrings. The earrings are both marked. The pin is 1½" in diameter and the earrings are 1¼" tall. **$200.00 – 225.00.** Author collection.

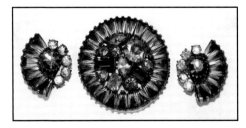

Claudette pinwheel set of pin and earrings in shades of blue, some stones with AB finish. The set has a gunmetal finish. The pin is 1¾" in diameter and the earrings are 1⅛". **$200.00 – 225.00.** Author collection.

Les Bernard set of articulated faux pearl flower with matching pearl earrings. This pin came in two sizes and this is the smaller size, measuring 2½" x 2" while the earrings are ⅞". All of the petals move to allow you to make a softly cupped flower bud or a fully opened blossom. All pieces are marked. **$250.00 – 275.00.** Author collection.

Les Bernard leaf pin with matching earrings. The leaf is set with marcasites and blue and green rhinestones, a Les Bernard innovation. The leaf is 2½" x 1" and the earrings are ⅞". Notice that the earrings are the same as the pearl earrings at left. All pieces are marked. **$100.00 – 125.00.** Author collection.

This Les Bernard leaf with matching earrings is set with a faux center pearl, marcasite, and multicolored cabochons. The pin is 2⅛" x 1¾" and the earrings are ⅞". All pieces are marked. **$100.00 – 125.00.** Author collection.

Here are the two sizes of the mechanical flower pins by Les Bernard, along with the matching earrings. The smaller pin is 2⅜" x 1½" while the larger flower is 3" x 2¼", fully extended. The earrings are both marked and ⅞". I love these pins and apparently can't get enough of them. **$450.00 – 500.00 for the set.** Author collection.

Trifari Etoilé pin and earrings set. This set was shown in a 1959 Trifari ad shown on page 171. It features pale canary yellow AB marquise rhinestones and what collectors call "lava rock" stones, accented by several tiny round rhinestones. Notice the earrings have pear-shaped stones. The back of this pin is beautifully finished and this set looks as if it were never worn. The pin is 2½" x 2⅛" and the earrings are ⅞" in diameter. All pieces are marked with "Trifari" and the small crown. **$250.00 – 275.00.** Author collection.

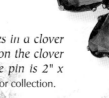

Rare Calvaire find of green glass heart-shaped stones in a clover design. The pin is signed "Calvaire" and "Sterling" on the clover stem. All stones are unfoiled and open backed. The pin is 2" x 1¼" and the earrings are ⅝". **$250.00 – 300.00.** Author collection.

This absolutely stunning Claudette set has large square red glass stones and the pin is accented with red and AB pink stones. The large red stones are unfoiled and open backed. Only the earrings are signed. The set is japanned. The pin is 2⅛" x 2⅛" and the earrings are ¾". **$200.00 – 250.00.** Author collection.

Claudette swirl design pin and earring set in gunmetal finish. The set has orange, green, and AB stones. The pin is 2" in diameter and the earrings are 1¼". **$200.00 – 225.00.** Author collection.

Claudette red and pink AB set in japanned setting. The pin with art glass stones is 2¼" x 2⅜" and the earrings are 1¼". **$200.00 – 225.00.** Author collection.

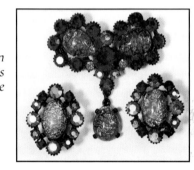

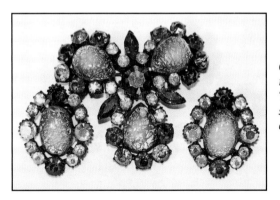

Claudette blue trefoil design pin with matching earrings. I featured the matching red set in my first book. The pin has art glass stones and regular and AB stones in a japanned setting. The pin is 2¼" and the earrings are 1¼". **$300.00 – 325.00.** Author collection.

This amazing green Claudette pin has two pairs of matching earrings. The pin is actually missing a teardrop-shaped green glass stone at the bottom. The pin is 2¼" x 1½" and the larger earrings are 1¼" tall. The setting is japanned and all of the earrings are marked. The missing drop is not noticeable and the set is still rare. **$225.00 – 275.00.** Author collection.

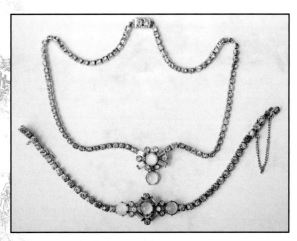

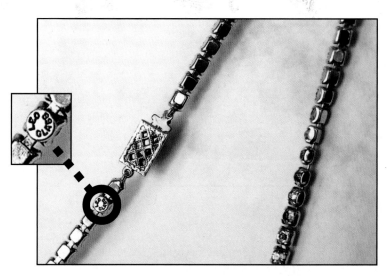

This set was purchased as an unsigned set with moonstones and clear rhinestones, but I saw the tiny Leo Glass mark on each piece near the clasps. The bracelet is 7" long and the necklace is 14½" long. The moonstones have an open back setting. **$350.00 – 375.00.** Author collection.

Reverse view showing signature.

Les Bernard set of two mechanical flower pins in both sizes with blue and green rhinestones, and matching earrings. All are signed. The large pin is 3", the smaller pin is 2½". **$450.00 – 500.00 for the set.** Author collection.

This ART set of necklace and bracelet has smoky topaz round stones accented with AB stones. The necklace is 16" long and the bracelet 7¼". Both are signed. The large round stones have an open back setting. **$95.00 – 125.00.** Author collection.

Black glass stones set of leaf-shaped pin with matching earrings. All stones are prong set. The set is unsigned. The pin is 2¼" and the earrings are 1½". **$55.00 – 65.00.** Author collection.

This pink cat's eye set of pin and earrings is unmarked. The pin is 2⅜" tall and the earrings are 1". **$65.00 – 75.00.** Author collection.

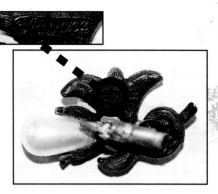

Here is an unusual unsigned set of clear gray rhinestones with clear and AB stones. The bracelet has unfoiled gray teardrop stones with an open back, and the earrings have gray unfoiled marquise stones with an open back. The bracelet is 7¼" long and the earrings are 1½". **$95.00 – 125.00.** Author collection.

This faux pearl necklace with matching earrings is signed "Ravana," an unusual name to find. I think the pendant looks like a stylized owl. Only one earring is signed. The pendant is 2¾" long with a 24" chain that may not be original, and the earrings are 1⅜". **$45.00 – 65.00.** Author collection.

View of Ravana signature on back of earring.

This stunning set in greens has a bracelet and matching earrings. None of the pieces are signed. The bracelet is 7½" and the earrings are 1½". **$150.00 – 175.00.** Author collection.

This pale pink faux pearl two-strand necklace with matching earrings is totally feminine. The necklace is 18" and the earrings are 1" in diameter. All are signed "Japan." **$65.00 – 75.00.** Carol Buckland collection.

Regency pin and earrings with cat's eye green cabochons accented with pale green rhinestones. **$135.00 – 165.00.** Carol Bell Treasures-In-Time collection.

Bronze rhinestones accent this coral and dark blue Vogue Jewelry pin and earrings set in a gold-tone setting. The pin is 2" x 1" and the earrings are 1¼" x ¾". **$125.00 – 145.00.** Carol Bell Treasures-In-Time collection.

This flower garden pin and earrings set is an original by Lawrence Vrba. The pin features dazzling flower blossoms on springs to give movement to the brooch. It has a wonderful variety of pinks and blues with some moonstones and some AB stones. It is handmade and signed with the Lawrence Vrba plaque. The brooch is 5½" x 3¼". The matching flower earrings with gigantic pink center stones measure 1⅜" in diameter and are both signed. **$500.00 – 600.00 for the set.** Barbara Wood collection.

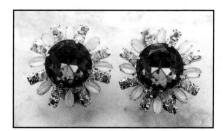

Matching earrings.

Necklaces

This necklace is unsigned but I believe it could be Trifari. It is made of links which each hold green, pink, and lavender glass cabochons and a faux pearl with clear rhinestones. This choker is 16" long and each link is 1¼" x 1". **$150.00 – 175.00.** Author collection.

This Miriam Haskell three-strand necklace features faux pearls and rhinestone spacers. This necklace is 14" long. **$345.00 – 365.00.** Carol Bell Treasures-In-Time collection.

This Miriam Haskell five-strand necklace features small turquoise colored glass beads with gold seed beads, and turquoise glass beads with blue crystal beads and gold seed beads. The clasp has dark blue rhinestones and crystal and turquoise glass beads. The necklace is 15½" long, the clasp is 1" and it is signed on the back. **$495.00 – 525.00.** Carol Bell Treasures-In-Time collection.

This beautiful necklace has faceted opal glass beads and purple glass flower beads. The unsigned necklace is 28" long. **$275.00 – 300.00.** Carol Bell Treasures-In-Time collection.

This gorgeous necklace has lavender rhinestones and four pendant drops with spiraling rhinestones each holding three purple glass cabochons. It is 17" long and drops are 4" long. **$400.00 – 450.00.** Carol Bell Treasures-In-Time collection.

This wonderful unsigned faux pearl necklace has gold rhinestones and blue and green glass beads. Notice the necklace is squared off at the bottom, instead of tapered. It is 15" long and has a hidden clasp. **$250.00 – 275.00.** Carol Bell Treasures-In-Time collection.

This lovely choker is made of cobalt and gold glass beads. Because of the design with the different shaped beads, it hangs beautifully. It is 16" long. **$375.00 – 425.00.** Carol Bell Treasures-In-Time collection.

This is an unsigned Schreiner necklace of clear rhinestones and faux pearls in a floral design. It is 14½" long. **$295.00 – 325.00.** Carol Bell Treasures-In-Time collection.

The beautiful necklace features clear and blue glass beads with a tassel of beads, which loops through the opposite side of the necklace. The beads are separated by rhinestone spacers. The necklace is 27" long and the tassel adds another 5". **$645.00 – 675.00.** Carol Bell Treasures-In-Time collection.

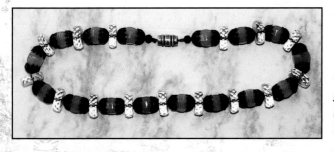

This French Art Deco necklace is made of green opalescent glass and clear crystal beads. This 19" long necklace is beautifully designed and heavy for its size. **$645.00 – 675.00.** Carol Bell Treasures-In-Time collection.

This Kramer necklace has large clear rhinestones set inside ornate flowered silver-tone settings. It is 16" long. **$150.00 – 225.00.** Carol Bell Treasures-In-Time collection.

Close-up view of Kramer necklace showing the elaborate settings.

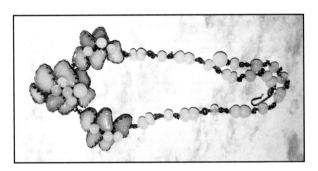

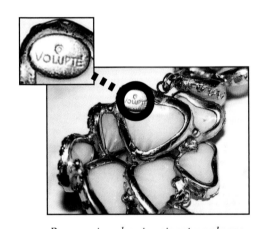

This beautiful floral Volupté necklace features molded white opalescent glass. Note the flowers are accented with glass beads. It measures 17". **$245.00 – 265.00.** Carol Bell Treasures-In-Time collection.

Reverse view showing signature plaque.

This gorgeous unsigned necklace has large marquise unfaceted stones enclosed in tiny cages giving the appearance of netting. It is similar to the line of caged jewelry done by Kramer. The stones outlining the design and the chain are gray. It is 16" long. **$125.00 – 145.00.** Barbara Wood collection.

Close-up view of necklace.

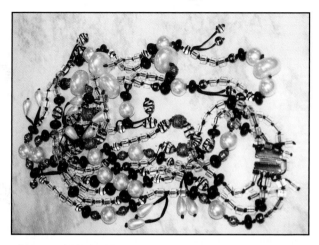

This incredible necklace has been attributed to Erik Beamon as a runway design. The shortest strand of the necklace is 45" long. The necklace has glass beads and faux pearls strung on black ribbon. **$500.00 – 575.00.** Carol Bell Treasures-In-Time collection.

This is a massive black bead necklace a with huge teardrop bead centerpiece. 19" long. **$125.00 – 175.00.** Carol Bell Treasures-In-Time collection.

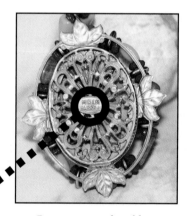

Miriam Haskell Egyptian scarab and beetle necklace with coral and turquoise colored glass beads. The pendant is 2½" long, while the necklace measures 19" long. As is **$245.00**, if perfect **$285.00.** Carol Bell Treasures-In-Time collection.

Reverse view of necklace showing signature.

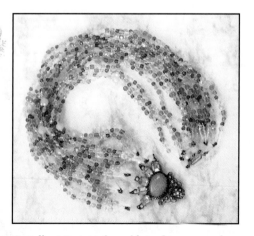

View showing clasp pendant.

Ornella 15-strand necklace has aqua, lavender, and topaz crystal beads, 16½" long. **$525.00 – 600.00.** Carol Bell Treasures-In-Time collection.

Here is the beautiful Elizabeth Taylor for Avon Forever Violet necklace from 1994. It has eight strands of amethyst glass beads and a clasp with rhinestones and faux pearls. The back is signed with a script "E" surrounded by the words "Elizabeth Taylor Avon." It is 18" long. **$100.00 – 125.00.** Barbara Wood collection.

This Italian glass bead necklace features banana bunches strung on wire with white speckled clear glass beads. Each tiny banana and leaf has its own wire and is hand wired onto the strand. It is 16" long. **$275.00 – 325.00.** Barbara Wood collection.

This unusual necklace is signed "Phyllis" and has clear and amethyst prong-set stones. It is a lariat style that fits over your head and is adjustable. The necklace is signed in a small plaque and is 18" long. **$65.00 – 85.00.** Author collection.

This rhinestone necklace is 31" long and is made from two strands of rhinestone chain twisted together. It is signed "Dauplaise." **$75.00 – 95.00.** Author collection.

With all of the vintage costume jewelry I own, these Mazer Bros. necklaces still remain some of my favorites. All of the necklaces and matching bracelets have the same clasp, so they are easily attached to one another, extending the length of any necklace to suit any outfit. I also take them and wind them twice around my wrist for a double strand bracelet. All of them are signed "Mazer Bros." on the back of the clasp and all of the clasps are set with four clear rhinestones. All stones are prong set, except on the clasp. The backs of the necklaces are as beautifully finished as the fronts. The first necklace features a stylized heart design holding a square center stone. The second one has wonderful round and baguette stones in the center. The third has a belt buckle type design. They range from 14½" to 15". **$150.00 – 175.00.** Author collection.

View showing mark on clasp.

Bracelets

Gorgeous Ciner hinged bangle bracelet covered with pavé rhinestones with red, green, and blue cabochons. **$535.00 – 565.00.** Carol Bell Treasures-In-Time collection.

View showing inside of bracelet with signature.

Here is an unsigned Hobé hinged bracelet with dangling beads in white and turquoise rhinestones. Many of these bracelets, like the wrap around designs from the same time period, were not signed, as they were sold with the parure and other pieces in the set were marked. This is one of the more fun Hobé bracelets to wear. **$225.00 – 250.00.** Carol Bell Treasures-In-Time collection.

This great Kramer bracelet has hot pink and pale blue rhinestones in an intricate design, and each rhinestone is prong set. The clasp is signed. The bracelet is 7½" long and ½" wide with a push-in clasp and a safety chain. **$295.00 – 325.00.** Carol Bell Treasures-In-Time collection.

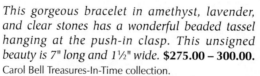

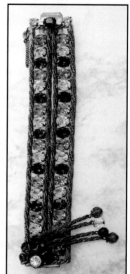

This gorgeous bracelet in amethyst, lavender, and clear stones has a wonderful beaded tassel hanging at the push-in clasp. This unsigned beauty is 7" long and 1½" wide. **$275.00 – 300.00.** Carol Bell Treasures-In-Time collection.

This is a beautiful Hollycraft bracelet with faux opal cabochons accented with clear rhinestones. It is 7" long and is signed. **$175.00 – 195.00.**

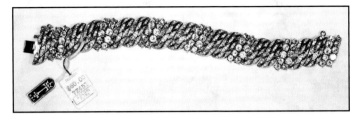

Trifari Trianon Art Deco look rhinestone bracelet with original tags. The original price was $60.00. **$245.00 – 275.00.** Carol Bell Treasures-In-Time collection.

This David Mandel yellow glass stone bangle bracelet is signed on edge. **$225.00 – 300.00.** Cordelia Meanor collection.

View of signature plaque on bracelet.

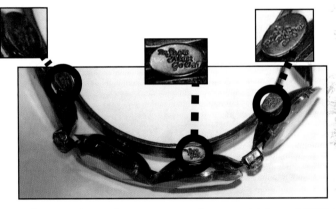

This David Mandel bangle bracelet has blue teardrop glass stones accented with topaz stones. **$225.00 – 300.00.** Cordelia Meanor collection.

Side view shows three signature plaques, which read "The Show Must Go On."

Matched pair of Marc Labat brown and ivory colored bangle bracelets. The bracelets are 1⅜" wide with a depth of ⅝". **$175.00 – 195.00 each.** Barbara Wood collection.

View of inside of bracelet with signature.

This Selro devil bracelet is actually quite beautiful in person. It has lovely cabochons and rhinestones and each devil is stamped "Selro" on the back. **$275.00 – 325.00.** Carol Bell Treasures-In-Time collection.

This Selro red devil link bracelet has dark red cabochons and ruby red rhinestones on each link. The bracelet is 7½" x 1¾". Each link is signed "Selro Corp." **$325.00 – 350.00.** Carol Bell Treasures-In-Time collection.

This Christian Dior by Kramer bracelet in gold-tone features clear rhinestones with a watch style link bracelet, 7¼". **$145.00 – 165.00.** Carol Bell Treasures-In-Time collection.

This Joseff silver-tone bracelet has eight chains and amethyst rhinestones. **$475.00 – 550.00.** Carol Bell Treasures-In-Time collection.

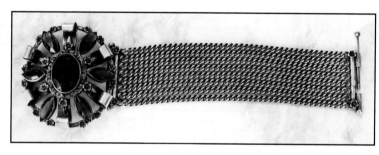

This Austrian bracelet was made by Schoffel and Co. and has deep blue and clear rhinestones. **$175.00 – 200.00.** Carol Bell Treasures-In-Time collection.

Reverse view of bracelet showing crown signature of Schoffel and Co.

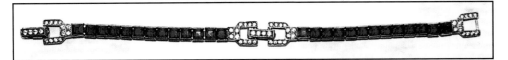

This wonderful deco sterling bracelet has two clasps that both work with clear and ruby red rhinestones. It is 6⅞" long. **$195.00 – 225.00.** Barbara Wood collection.

Hollycraft bracelet with pale blue, clear, and AB clear rhinestones. The bracelet is marked "Hollycraft COPR." and what I believe is the date of 1957, it is difficult to make out clearly. The bracelet is 7¼". **$85.00 – 95.00.** Author collection.

This is a bracelet that takes your breath away in person. It is signed "Mazer Bros." and has emerald green glass cabochons accented with clear rhinestones. The design mimics genuine jewelry. It is 7" long. **$200.00 – 250.00.** Author collection.

Glamorous Claudette bracelet with bright clear rhinestones. This bracelet is signed and is 7" long. **$95.00 – 125.00.** Author collection.

Claudette silver-tone bracelet with faux half pearls and blue rhinestones. I have also seen this set with red stones and with brown stones. The bracelet is marked on the clasp and is 7¼" long. **$45.00 – 65.00.** Author collection.

Here is something you probably haven't seen before, a lovely faux pearl bracelet signed "Tortolani." It has large baroque pearls and small pearls in what looks like grape clusters. The bracelet is signed on the back of the first link and is 8" long. **$95.00 – 125.00.** Author collection.

Close-up view of signature.

This rhinestone bangle bracelet with beautiful sapphire blue and clear baguette stones is signed "Urgnani." I have researched the signature to no avail, but believe it could be Italian. It has an applied signature plaque which appears complete and the signature clearly reads "URGNANI." **$125.00 – 150.00.** Author collection.

This Regency bracelet features turquoise colored flat stones and large blue AB and lavender glass stones. The bracelet is marked "Regency" on the back of the stone holding the ring for the safety chain. It is 7¼". **$175.00 – 200.00.** Author collection.

This bracelet has clear glass oval stones as links with two tiny clear rhinestone accents. It is unsigned and is 7" with a push-in clasp. The stones are unfoiled and open back. **$85.00 – 120.00.** Author collection.

Unsigned bracelet with pink marquise stones and pink and white givré stones. All the stones are unfoiled and open backed. The bracelet has push-in clasp and is 7" long. **$95.00 – 125.00.** Author collection.

This wonderful pot metal hinged-cuff bracelet has a large glass ruby cabochon center stone and has clear rhinestones all the way around the bracelet. There is also a safety chain. The bracelet is not signed. **$95.00 – 125.00.** Author collection.

This Goldette N.Y. bracelet looks like a Victorian slide bracelet, but the links do not move. Each link is set with a smoke colored rhinestone. The bracelet is 7" long. **$85.00 – 120.00.** Author collection.

This is a Joseph Gourdji cuff bracelet with mask wearing a clear rhinestone headpiece. The cuff is larger at the top to fit better around the wrist. The cuff is 4⅜" tall and has the Gourdji signature on the back. It is an original piece of art. **$150.00 – 175.00.** Barbara Wood collection.

This Judy Lee clear rhinestone bracelet with its original box is signed on the clasp and is 7⅛" long. **$50.00 – 65.00.** Author collection.

This Rebajes Modernist coil copper cuff is 2" wide. The cuff is signed on front edge. **$270.00 – 325.00.** Barbara Wood collection.

View showing signature.

This Rebajes copper cuff bracelet is 2" wide and is signed on front edge. **$195.00 – 225.00.** Barbara Wood collection.

This Rebajes fleur de lis copper cuff is 2" wide and is signed on front edge of cuff. **$250.00 – 275.00.** Barbara Wood collection.

This bracelet for pink lovers by Larry Vrba has large square pink stones outlined with large emerald cut stones. It is made for today's woman with a length of 8" and is 1" wide. **$155.00 – 175.00.** Karen Bird collection.

A bracelet fit for a queen, this Larry Vrba design has soft pale yellow stones and clear stones, the pale yellow stones at the edges are foiled and open backed. It is 8" x 2⅛". **$230.00 – 260.00.** Karen Bird collection.

This Hobé art glass bracelet with green plastic beads strung on a chain is 7½" though part of that is due to the stretching of the chain. Notice this bracelet is adjustable like their necklaces, plus it has bead dangles. **$150.00 – 175.00.** Author collection.

Brooches and Pins

Miriam Haskell pearl appeal with baroque pearls in a gilt setting. This is a typical Haskell design that collectors know and love. It is 2" x 2". **$295.00 – 325.00.** Carol Bell Treasures-In-Time collection.

Beautiful Hattie Carnegie poured glass pin with dark red, medium blue, and dark green poured glass accented with clear rhinestones. It is 1½" x 1½" and is signed on the back. The stones are open backed. **$250.00 – 295.00.** Carol Bell Treasures-In-Time collection.

This Josef Morton pin with pale green and pale blue glass pieces wired in place is signed on the back. It is 2" in diameter. **$135.00 – 150.00.** Carol Bell Treasures-In-Time collection.

This purple and dark green pin is great for Mardi Gras, with dangling beads in the center. The unsigned pin is 2" x 2½". **$245.00 – 265.00.** Carol Bell Treasures-In-Time collection.

This contemporary Miriam Haskell gilt leaf and flower pin with glass leaves and rhinestone is probably from the 1970s. **$220.00 – 245.00.** Carol Bell Treasures-In-Time collection.

Reverse view of pin with signature plaque.

Fabulous Miriam Haskell pin with hand-wired seed beads and large faux pearls on dangling chains. Notice the bottom of each pearl is accented with a seed bead. The chains hang from gilt pierced metal beads that have been covered with seed beads. It is 5" tall and 2¾" wide. **$395.00 – 425.00.** Carol Bell Treasures-In-Time collection.

Reverse view of pin.

This unsigned Schreiner oval domed pin has bright aqua cabochon stones and rhinestones in a gunmetal finish. It is 2½" x 2" and sits 1" high, with open back unfoiled stones. **$225.00 – 240.00.** Carol Bell Treasures-In-Time collection.

Reverse view of pin.

Unsigned Schreiner pin with black rhinestones. If you look closely you will see the flower and leaf design. The pin is 2¼" in diameter and 1" high. **$245.00 – 265.00.** Carol Bell Treasures-In-Time collection.

Schreiner New York floral pin in clear and smoky rhinestones in a japanned setting. Three of the flowers stand above the rest like tremblers and can spin. The pin is 3¼" x 2". **$295.00 – 325.00.** Carol Bell Treasures-In-Time collection.

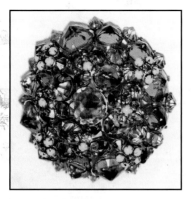

Schreiner New York pin in smoky topaz with tiny flowers in turquoise and peridot colored rhinestones. It is 2½" in diameter. **$425.00 – 450.00.** Carol Bell Treasures-In-Time collection.

Unsigned Schreiner pin in shades of blues, with large rhinestones mounted below smaller ones. Typical Schreiner construction. It is 2" x 1¾". **$215.00 – 225.00.** Carol Bell Treasures-In-Time collection.

Side view of unsigned Schreiner pin showing height of pin.

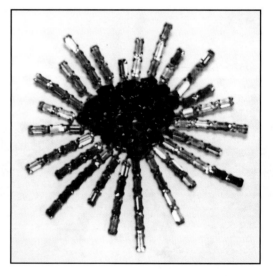

It is very difficult to photograph this Schreiner New York beauty; it is a sunburst ruffle pin with inverted amber stones surrounded by clear baguette stones. This large pin is 3¼" in diameter. **$475.00 – 495.00.** Carol Bell Treasures-In-Time collection.

This amazing pendant/pin is attributed to Schreiner. It has beautiful cabochon stones in a variety of colors surrounding a large faux pearl, in a gunmetal finish. It is 3⅓" x 3". **$425.00 – 450.00.** Carol Bell Treasures-In-Time collection.

Reverse view of pin.

Pink and gray unsigned Schreiner pin with a pale green center stone. It is 3" in diameter. **$295.00 – 325.00.** Carol Bell Treasures-In-Time collection.

Extraordinary unsigned Schreiner pendant/pin with clear rhinestones and Lucite crystals. The pin measures 5" tall by 3⅝" wide. **$395.00 – 425.00.** Carol Bell Treasures-In-Time collection.

Fashioncraft Robert heart pin with pink and blue rhinestones. The rhinestones spill out of the heart on individual wires. 2" x 1¾". **$125.00 – 145.00.** Carol Bell Treasures-In-Time collection.

This mask pin, signed "Fashioncraft Robert" has mesh hair and a rhinestone headdress. This rare pin's gold finish shows it was a well loved treasure. The signature is a half moon shape with Fashioncraft in upper case letters around the top of the moon shape and robert in lower case letters straight across the straight edge of the bottom of the moon shape. 2" x 2½". **$295.00 – 325.00.** Carol Bell Treasures-In-Time collection.

Reverse view of pin.

Schiaparelli shocking pink pin with large center stones. 2¾" x 1½". **$325.00 – 350.00.** Carol Bell Treasures-In-Time collection.

Schiaparelli shield-shaped pin with dark green, amber, blue and clear rhinestones in a gold-tone setting. All of the stones are unfoiled and set open back. 2" x 2½". **$295.00 – 325.00.** Carol Bell Treasures-In-Time collection.

Elegant Schiaparelli swirl pin with dark blue cabochon center stones, accented with pale blue baguette and clear rhinestones. 3" x 1¼". **$175.00 – 200.00.** Carol Bell Treasures-In-Time collection.

This Miriam Haskell pin is a Robert Clark design from the 1960s. It features blue glass stones with faux opals and is accented with clear rhinestones. The pin is signed with the horseshoe-shaped mark on the back, and measures 2½" x 1½". **$275.00 – 300.00.** Carol Bell Treasures-In-Time collection.

Reverse view of pin showing signature plaque.

Miriam Haskell gold-tone leaf pin with rose montees hand wired around the edges of the leaves. It is signed in raised letters on an oval plaque. 2¾" long. **$285.00 – 300.00.** Carol Bell Treasures-In-Time collection.

The golden daisies in this Miriam Haskell pin have faux pearl centers. This pin is signed in raised letters in an oval plaque. 3" wide. **$285.00 – 300.00.** Carol Bell Treasures-In-Time collection.

The bud is opening on this Miriam Haskell flower pin in pink and amethyst. The bud has a large art glass stone and pink rhinestones outline the petals. The pin is signed in raised letters in an oval plaque. **$375.00 – 395.00.** Carol Bell Treasures-In-Time collection.

This Miriam Haskell beauty features ruby red art glass, red seed beads, and clear rhinestones rondelles. It is signed in raised letters on an oval plaque. It measures 3" across and is breathtaking in person and very difficult to capture with a camera. **$500.00 – 575.00.** Carol Bell Treasures-In-Time collection.

Lovely Miriam Haskell gilt bar pin with a variety of faux pearls. 3½" x ¾". **$275.00 – 300.00.** Carol Bell Treasures-In-Time collection.

This Miriam Haskell flower pin with a pearl center features petals outlined with red rhinestones. The center pearl is outlined with citrine rhinestones. 2⅜" in diameter. **$345.00 – 365.00.** Carol Bell Treasures-In-Time collection.

KJL domed pin features purple, green, and dark red Lucite cabochons surrounding a large amber glass center stone. It is accented with small clear rhinestones. Note the cabochons are squared with corners, quite unusual. The pin is 2¾" x 2½" and sits quite high. It is signed on the back in an oval plaque. **$425.00 – 465.00.** Carol Bell Treasures-In-Time collection.

Kramer domed prong set red rhinestone pin. 2" in diameter and 1¼" deep. **$85.00 – 95.00.** Carol Bell Treasures-In-Time collection.

This unsigned dolphin pin looks like a Kenneth Lane design. Pavé stones cover the head and tail, while black enamel forms the scales, a large faux pearl dangles from the dolphin's mouth. 4" x 2½". **$345.00 – 375.00.** Carol Bell Treasures-In-Time collection.

Rare Brania pin with faux pearls, faux turquoise, clear rhinestones and marbled green marquise stones. 2¾" in diameter. **$175.00 – 195.00.** Carol Bell Treasures-In-Time collection.

This very large Ciner floral pin in gold-tone is accented with clear rhinestones and white cabochons, and it measures 4¼" x 2½". **$275.00 – 295.00.** Carol Bell Treasures-In-Time collection.

This Ciner domed pin/pendant is set with clear rhinestones and a faux pearl center, accented with colored glass cabochons. 2" in diameter. **$155.00 – 175.00.** Carol Bell Treasures-In-Time collection.

Reverse view of pin showing depth and pendant bale.

Coro Craft sterling gold-washed enameled flower pin with blue center stone and clear rhinestone accents. The pin is signed "Coro Craft" and "Sterling" and is 2" in diameter, with center stone being ½" wide. **$145.00 – 165.00.** Carol Bell Treasures-In-Time collection.

Boucher interprets the stars with this pin featuring amethyst cabochons with clear rhinestones in the center and as accents. The pin is signed with "Boucher" and the design number. **$125.00 – 145.00.** Carol Bell Treasures-In-Time collection.

Shade of blue illuminate this Regency pin in a japanned setting. Look closely to see the center teardrop shapes in molded glass. 2⅝" x 2¼". **$110.00 – 125.00.** Carol Bell Treasures-In-Time collection.

Ruby red glass drops highlight this gorgeous Regency pin accented with AB red rhinestones. 2¼" x 1¾". **$100.00 – 125.00.** Carol Bell Treasures-In-Time collection.

This Chinese water boy with his cloisonné water carriers is signed on the back with Chinese characters. This large pin measures 3½" x 3". **$135.00 – 155.00.** Carol Bell Treasures-In-Time collection.

Reverse view of pin showing Chinese characters signature plaque.

This Mimi di N pin has red and clear rhinestones and faux turquoise cabochons. It is 3½" long and is signed. **$275.00 – 295.00.** Carol Bell Treasures-In-Time collection.

This Langani pink art glass beaded pin is not signed but has the signature black bead hidden in the beading. It is from the 1960s and is 2½" long. **$145.00 – 165.00.** Carol Bell Treasures-In-Time collection.

Reverse view showing black bead.

This Miriam Haskell white seed bead and milk glass pin is 3" tall. **$350.00 – 395.00.** Carol Bell Treasures-In-Time collection.

This Jomaz stylized bow has sapphire and clear rhinestones. It is 2⅞" x 1⅝" and is signed. **$245.00 – 275.00.** Carol Bell Treasures-In-Time collection.

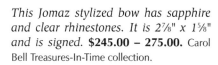

Ornella pin with faux pearls and green glass beads, 2" in diameter. **$200.00 – 225.00.** Carol Bell Treasures-In-Time collection.

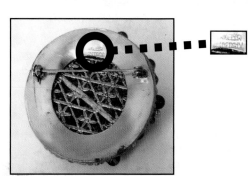

Reverse view of pin showing stamped signature.

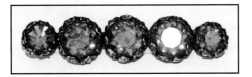

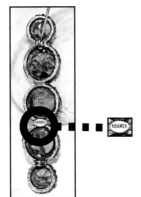

Kramer bar pin in gold-tone setting with large green glass stones, 3¼". **$75.00 – 95.00.** Carol Bell Treasures-In-Time collection.

Reverse view of pin showing signature.

Kramer bar pin in gold-tone setting with large clear glass stones, 3¼". **$65.00 – 85.00.** Carol Bell Treasures-In-Time collection.

Headlight pin in gold-tone setting with enormous clear glass stones, 2½". **$125.00 – 150.00.** Carol Bell Treasures-In-Time collection.

Unsigned gold-tone enameled mandolin with turquoise and clear accents and two dangling chains. The pin is very dimensional and measures 3" x 1¼". **$95.00 – 115.00.** Carol Bell Treasures-In-Time collection.

Beautiful French pin with blue glass dangles and prong-set clear rhinestones. 2½" x 2¼". **$200.00 – 275.00.** Carol Bell Treasures-In-Time collection.

Fashioncraft by Robert "V" for victory pin with red, clear, and blue rhinestones. **$150.00 – 175.00.** Carol Bell Treasures-In-Time collection.

This unsigned flower japanned pin has heart-shaped stones as the petals. 3" x 2½". **$150.00 – 200.00.** Carol Bell Treasures-In-Time collection.

This pin of a demure lady peeking from behind a curtain was made by Sergio Bustamante and is signed with his name, ©, and MEX 925. 1¾" x 2". Sergio Bustamante is an internationally well known papier maché artist who was born in Culiacan, Sinaloa, Mexico, and who now lives in Guadalajara. His art work is sought after by collectors around the world. **$595.00 – 650.00.** Barbara Wood collection.

Halloween is more fun with cats in costume! This pin is signed "A.J.C." and is 1½" x 2". **$65.00 – 75.00.** Barbara Wood collection.

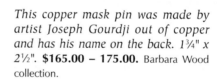

This copper mask pin was made by artist Joseph Gourdji out of copper and has his name on the back. 1¾" x 2½". **$165.00 – 175.00.** Barbara Wood collection.

This monkey is trying to steal some coconuts from this rhinestone and enameled tree. 2¾" x 2¼". This was a very popular pin and is seen in a variety of finishes, some with more rhinestones, some with less; some with more enameling, some with less. **$165.00 – 175.00.** Barbara Wood collection.

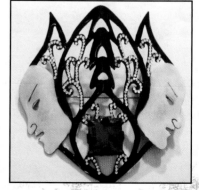

Gourdji double face pin with large square red stone, 4" x 4". **$225.00 – 250.00.** Barbara Wood collection.

Gourdji swan kissing a lady pin with clear, blue, and orange rhinestones, 3½" wide. **$250.00 – 275.00.** Barbara Wood collection.

This beautiful circle pin mimics genuine jewelry and is unsigned, but looks like Mazer or Trifari. 2" x 1¼". The back of the pin is beautifully finished. **$55.00 – 75.00.** Author collection.

This Jeanne tree pin has crystal bead dangles, is accented with clear rhinestones, and is signed "Jeanne" with the © copyright symbol. 2⅛" x 2". **$65.00 – 85.00.** Author collection.

Reverse view of tree showing signature.

This HAR enameled flower looks like a dogwood blossom but it has one too many petals. The center has pale orange rhinestones. It is 2¼" x 2¼" and is signed "HAR" on the back. **$55.00 – 75.00.** Author collection.

Reverse view showing signature.

Bob Mackie harlequin pin has his left leg attached to dance. His enameled body is accented with pink rhinestones. 2⅝" tall. **$85.00 – 110.00.** Author collection.

This Calvaire pin has large pear-shaped amethyst glass stones and the stem is filled with graduating emerald-shaped clear stones. The pin is signed "Calvaire" and is 2¼" tall. **$300.00 – 325.00.** Author collection.

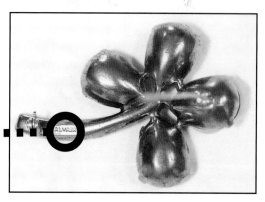

Reverse view of pin showing signature.

This heavy gold-tone Calvaire budding flower pin is accented with clear stones on the edges of two of the petals. It is signed "Calvaire" and is 2¾" tall. **$125.00 – 150.00.** Author collection.

This wonderful tree is a Graziano design with dangling rhinestones hidden among the branches. The leaves are set with coordinating colors of rhinestones. 2¼" x 2". **$65.00 – 85.00.** Author collection.

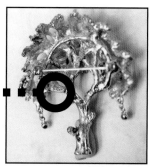

Reverse view showing signature.

Fun little enameled roadrunner pin signed "J. J." 2" long. **$25.00 – 35.00.** Author collection.

This is something I promise you will not see anywhere else. It is a one-of-a-kind Dotty Stringfield design made exclusively for me. I call this Christmas tree pin "Everything's Bigger In Texas" because it is a whopping 6¼" tall, and it is covered with symbols of Texas. It even has wonderful dangles to make lovely music. Every time I wear this pin I am asked where I got it. It is signed "Dorothea" and it has a bale to allow you to wear it on a chain. Dotty's website can be found at www.illusionjewels.com and my first book gives detailed information about her site. **$150.00 – 195.00.** Author collection.

This Christmas tree pin was made by another Texan. This pink tree was made by beegee mcbride whose website can be found at www.southtexastrading.com and her website information can be found in my first book. The pin is signed "beegee" and is 2¾" tall. **$65.00 – 75.00.** Author collection.

Coro bird in flight pin with clear rhinestones. It is signed "Coro Reg. Pat. Pend." and is 1⅝". **$95.00 – 125.00.** Author collection.

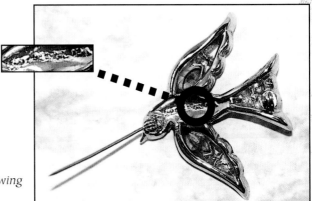

Reverse view showing signature.

This Austrian pin has beautiful clear rhinestones which are all prong set. It is signed "Made in Austria" on the back and is 2" in diameter. **$30.00 – 45.00.** Author collection.

This exquisite bow design is by Hattie Carnegie. It has prong-set clear rhinestones and two baroque pearl dangles. 4½" long. A classic design. **$150.00 – 175.00.** Author collection.

Side view showing bee.

This happy little Coro daisy pin has a bee trembling over the top. 2¼" in diameter. **$25.00 – 45.00.** Author collection.

This adorable little fish is attached to her family who float in a glass bubble above her head. Inside the bubble are three gold fish, some tiny bubbles, and some sea weed. The fish is 1¼" and the bubble is ⅞" in diameter. **$125.00 – 150.00.** Author collection.

Reverse view of pins.

Wonderfully articulated Don-Lin bucking bronco cowboy on horse pin under a half moon. This great little enameled pin is 4" tall. $55.00 – 65.00. Author collection.

This mink poodle sweater guard has the front and back end of the poodle covered with mink. The front end wears a lovely black cabochon. The rhinestone chain is 3½" long and the poodle is nearly 3" high. **$15.00 – 25.00.** Author collection.

This pair of Claudette scatter pins with green and clear rhinestones is shown on its original card. The pins measure 1" each and neither is signed. **$65.00 – 80.00.** Author collection.

Iridescent blues leaf pin signed "ART." This pin has AB marquise unfaceted stones and clear stones and light sky blue marquise stones. 3⅜" x 2¼". **$85.00 – 95.00.** Author collection.

Reverse view showing signature.

Faux pearl and enameled pin with clear rhinestones. This gold-tone pin is 2⅜" in diameter and is signed with an "X" and "SMB," which is the mark of Sandra Miller Burrows. Her jewelry is quite rare. **$65.00 – 85.00.** Author collection.

Ladies' pearl boot pin by Ornella, marked "Ornella Made Italy." The pearls are hand wired on with tiny AB stones as accents. 2" wide and 2¼" tall. **$155.00 – 175.00.** Author collection.

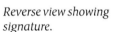

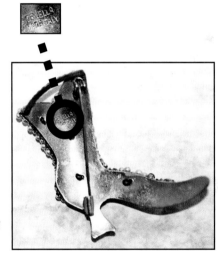

Reverse view showing signature.

Here is a fabulous little zebra pin in sterling with a gold wash. He has green rhinestones and a little red eye and is signed "Sterling" but has no other marks. 2¾" x 1¾". **$150.00 – 175.00.** Author collection.

Here is a great dangle pin that is signed "Sterling C. R. Co." This is a hard mark to find. 3" tall. There is a tiny bale allowing the pin to be worn as a pendant. **$95.00 – 125.00.** Author collection.

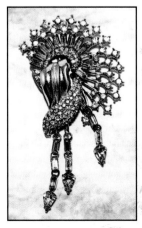

This bow-type pin has a plastic center stone and the back is signed "Kim" in script. Nothing is known yet about this company but its jewelry suggests a time frame of the 1970s or the 1980s. The pin is nearly 4" wide. **$25.00 – 40.00.** Author collection.

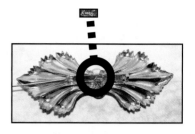

Reverse view showing signature.

This gold-tone flower pin with clear rhinestones is marked "K of B '62." 3½" tall. **$55.00 – 75.00.** Author collection.

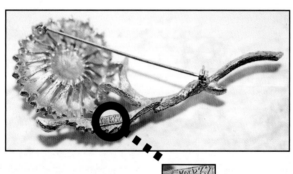

Reverse view showing signature.

A beautiful copper floral offering from Joseph Gourdji in the shape of a red flower with clear rhinestone accents. There is a bale attached to allow you to wear it as a necklace. It is 2½" in diameter and is signed "Gourdji." **$95.00 – 125.00.** Author collection.

Mazer flower pin with blue rhinestone petals and clear rhinestones. The blue stones are unfoiled and open backed. The pin is signed "Mazer" and is 2½" tall. **$95.00 – 125.00.** Author collection.

Here is a beautiful example of a clear rhinestone pin from the 1940s. It has larger than usual stones. 3½" x 2". **$150.00 – 175.00.** Barbara Wood collection.

Circus performer elephant with pavé clear stones and a green eye, 1¾". There is a mark on the back which looks like either an "A" inside a triangle or two triangles. **$85.00 – 95.00.** Barbara Wood collection.

This distinctive pin features unfoiled oval deep purple glass stones. They are open backed. 1⅝" in diameter. **$65.00 – 75.00.** Barbara Wood collection.

This remarkable little pin in shades of blue has rhinestones and dangling beads. The royal blue center stone is foiled and open backed. All stones are prong set. 2⅞" long. **$75.00 – 85.00.** Barbara Wood collection.

This large silver-tone pin is signed "Schreiner New York." It has faceted purple glass stones and pink cabochons. All the stones are unfoiled and open backed except for the center stone, where the signature plaque has been placed. The pin also has two bales for attaching to a chain to wear as a necklace. 3½" x 3". **$165.00 – 195.00.** Barbara Wood collection.

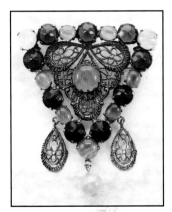

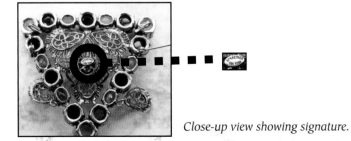

Close-up view showing signature.

Hot pink celluloid flower pin embedded with clear rhinestones. 3⅝" long. **$65.00 – 95.00.** Barbara Wood collection.

This Penguin jelly belly pin is 2" tall and marked "Sterling." **$75.00 – 85.00.** Barbara Wood collection.

Talk about making a statement — this enormous pin has amethyst, light pink, and dark pink stones accented with pink marbled glass cabochons. The pin is unsigned and 3⅛" in diameter. The large oval foiled amethyst stones and the small round unfoiled light pink stones are open backed. **$55.00 – 75.00.** Barbara Wood collection.

This Dorothy Bauer brightly colored kite pin has a sweet little rhinestone chain tail. The kite has rows of red, orange, peridot, and medium blue stones outlining a clear center stone. The pin is 4¼" including tail and is signed "Bauer" on a plaque on the back. **$75.00 – 85.00.** Barbara Wood collection.

A dog howling at the moon is a Southwestern motif, especially when rendered in turquoise blue colored rhinestones. This little guy has a blue eye and a little black nose. It measures 2⅝" x 2⅜" and has the Bauer signature plaque on the back. It is also a limited edition. **$75.00 – 85.00.** Barbara Wood collection.

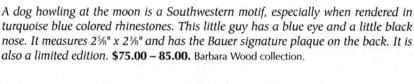

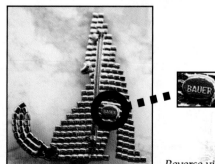

Reverse view showing signature.

Talk about bold! This bright and stunning pin with large round stones resembling a grape cluster was made in the 1960s by Vogue. The largest stones are ¾" wide, the pin measures 3¼" x 2½". **$120.00 – 175.00.** Barbara Wood collection.

Reverse view showing signature.

Another bold Vogue design from the 1960s, this pin also has ¾" stones. Both pins have a small signature plaque on the back, and this one is 2" in diameter. **$95.00 – 120.00.** Barbara Wood collection.

This whimsical dragon pin has red and blue rhinestones and is 3½" x 2". **$125.00 – 150.00.** Barbara Wood collection.

This large bird is taking a respite from the day's endeavors. He is marked "Sterling" and has a large topaz glass stone body and a small topaz eye, and his upraised wings are accented with clear stones. The center stone is unfoiled and open backed. Pin is 3" x 2¾". **$130.00 – 155.00.** Barbara Wood collection.

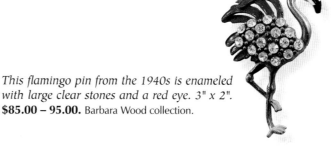

This flamingo pin from the 1940s is enameled with large clear stones and a red eye. 3" x 2". **$85.00 – 95.00.** Barbara Wood collection.

Another 1940s flamingo pin with enameling and red rhinestones with a clear stone eye. 3" x 2". **$125.00 – 145.00.** Barbara Wood collection.

This 1940s flamingo pin has green enameling, green rhinestones, and a red stone eye. 3⅛" x 2". **$125.00 – 150.00.** Barbara Wood collection.

Reverse view of pin.

Here is an unsigned Coro flying bird from the 1940s. The pot-metal bird is enameled with a rhinestone neck and measures 3" x 2⅝". **$120.00 – 145.00.** Barbara Wood collection.

This striking leaf pin with prong-set blue rhinestones and clear glued-in stones is signed "Sonia Lee Sterling" on the back. The pin is from the 1940s and measures 3¼" x 1½". **$65.00 – 95.00.** Barbara Wood collection.

Reverse view showing signature.

Unsigned bird on a branch pin from the 1940s, I have seen this pin signed with Made USA which was the mark on José Rodriguez and marked Trifari. This pin is enameled with rhinestones, including a teensy red stone eye. 2¼" x 1¾". **$60.00 – 75.00.** Barbara Wood collection.

Here is another 1940s pot-metal bird pin with enameling and rhinestones. 4⅜" long. **$70.00 – 85.00.** Barbara Wood collection.

This Coro Sterling four leaf clover pin with a very large pale blue emerald cut plastic center stone is in exceptional condition. 3" in diameter. **$100.00 – 125.00.** Barbara Wood collection.

I love this little Erwin Pearl bee with his trembling wing. He is signed "E. Pearl" with the © copyright symbol on the back of the stationary wing. He is enameled with pavé stones on his body and his wings. Pin is 2¼" tall. **$85.00 – 100.00.** Barbara Wood collection.

This Erwin Pearl mum pin with clear rhinestone center is signed "E. Pearl" with the © copyright symbol and is very realistic. 1⅞" in diameter. **$125.00 – 145.00.** Barbara Wood collection.

Reverse view showing signature.

This amusing little parasol pin has leaves and rhinestone flowers on the spokes. It is a Warner pin made in the 1950s and it is signed on the parasol handle. Note the three small rhinestones on the bottom front of the handle are in front of the pin clasp. 4³⁄₈" x 2⁷⁄₈". **$150.00 – 175.00.** Barbara Wood collection.

Reverse view showing signature.

This is an unmarked Kenneth Lane horse pin with multiple colored rhinestones in a gold-tone setting. 2" wide. **$95.00 – 115.00.** Barbara Wood collection.

This pin reveals the humorous side of Lawrence Vrba with the see, hear, and say no evil monkeys resting atop a banana tree. The design is more of a coconut tree but who can deny that those are ripe bananas hanging below the fronds? Brooch is over 5" tall and rhinestones wrap around the entire tree truck. **$395.00 – 450.00.** Barbara Wood collection.

View showing pin standing.

This is Larry Vrba's interpretation of a cross with a huge clear center stone surrounded by deep purple plastic stones and outlined with clear stones. This pin also has a bale attached to allow the owner to wear it as a pendant. 3⁵⁄₈" x 3¼". **$175.00 – 225.00.** Barbara Wood collection.

This beautiful Trifari panther is from the early 1970s and is covered with clear rhinestones. The pin is marked "Trifari" on the back and measures 2½" x 1⁷⁄₈". **$180.00 – 200.00.** Barbara Wood collection.

Earrings

These Miriam Haskell gilt earrings feature amber and citrine colored rhinestones. **$155.00 – 170.00.** Carol Bell Treasures-In-Time collection.

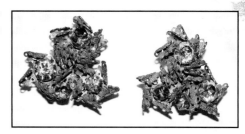

These beautiful sapphire blue and clear rhinestone earrings look genuine. They are made by Hattie Carnegie. Both earrings are signed and they are 1¼" x ⅝". **$175.00 – 195.00.** Carol Bell Treasures-In-Time collection.

These Schiaparelli earrings have large lemon and lime colored rhinestones. The setting is open behind all of the stones. 1½" in diameter. **$195.00 – 225.00.** Carol Bell Treasures-In-Time collection.

Beautiful blue/green Schiaparelli earrings. 1¼" x 1". **$125.00 – 145.00.** Carol Bell Treasures-In-Time collection.

Fabulous pair of beaded Jonne earrings with lavender glass beads, some with an AB finish. They are slightly over 1" in diameter. **$45.00 – 65.00.** Author collection.

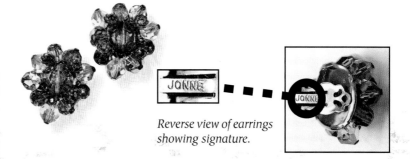

Reverse view of earrings showing signature.

Amazing pair of Claudette earrings in a gunmetal finish with large red and amethyst rhinestones. The amethyst ones are prong set but the red ones are not. **$75.00 – 100.00.** Author collection.

Both of these Claudette earrings in red and pink with marquise and round rhinestones are marked. They have a gunmetal finish and are 1¼" x 1⅛". **$75.00 – 100.00.** Author collection.

These little Warner earrings match the line of Warner red fruit jewelry. The earrings are both signed and are ¾" in diameter. **$55.00 – 65.00.** Author collection.

Reverse view showing signature.

The pearls in these beautiful faux pearl earrings in a triangle design are two different colors. The earrings are not marked and are 1" tall. **$25.00 – 35.00.** Author collection.

These lovely flower earrings are both signed "Sterling" and have screw-on backs. They have beautiful topaz prong-set stones. ⅞" in diameter. **$35.00 – 45.00.** Author collection.

These Les Bernard clip-on earrings have large deep green teardrop stones accented by clear rhinestones. The earrings are 1½" wide and only one is signed. **$30.00 – 45.00.** Author collection.

Claudette shades of blue earrings in a swirl design. Some of the stones have an AB finish. The earrings are 1⅜" tall. They are both signed and have a gunmetal finish. **$55.00 – 75.00.** Author collection.

These Claudette blue button style earrings have clear stone accents. The earrings are both signed and measure ⅞" in diameter. **$35.00 – 50.00.** Author collection.

These orange and amber earrings are signed "Sandor" which is a rare name to find. These earrings have a tiny faux pearl accent and both are signed. 1¼" tall. **$85.00 – 95.00.** Author collection.

Reverse view showing signature.

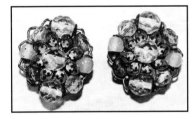

De Mario blue glass beaded earrings with rhinestone accents. The earrings are 1¼" and both are signed "De Mario N.Y." **$65.00 – 85.00.** Author collection.

These jade earrings are marked "Winard" and "1 / 20 12 kt. G.F." They are clip on and are 1¼" long. Winard usually used genuine materials such as cultured pearls and ivory, in addition to jade. **$15.00 – 20.00.** Author collection.

Plastic clip-on earrings with clear rhinestones. The earrings are unsigned and are 1⅜" long. **$15.00 – 20.00.** Author collection.

How much fun are these clip-on earrings? They are clear crackle glass marbles in a pronged setting. The earrings are unsigned and approximately ¾". **$15.00 – 20.00.** Author collection.

Blue plastic flower earrings with royal blue rhinestone centers. They are screw-on backs and are unsigned. They are 1¼". **$5.00 – 10.00.** Author collection.

These milk glass clip-on earrings from Western Germany have rhinestone ball dangles. They are both signed "Made in Western Germany" and are 1½" tall. **$10.00 – 15.00.** Author collection.

These amber rhinestone earrings look like they have ears of corn in the design. They are signed "STAR" and are 1" in diameter. **$25.00 – 40.00.** Author collection.

Bold clip-on earrings with prong set clear rhinestones. They are unsigned and sit very high as they resemble half of a ball. They are 1" in diameter. **$35.00 – 45.00.** Author collection.

Unsigned prong-set clear rhinestone clip-on earrings. These are beautifully designed. 1⅜" x 1". **$35.00 – 45.00.** Author collection.

These Trifari clip-on earrings have pale blue oval rhinestones accented with clear stone. 1" tall. **$15.00 – 30.00.** Author collection.

This pair of crown Trifari earrings has smoke-colored stones and clear stones accenting faux pearl centers. The clip-on earrings are 1" tall. **$35.00 – 45.00.** Author collection.

These clip-on earrings have green art glass beads with crystal beads and rhinestone rondelles, in addition to a silver-tone bead. 1½" tall. **$10.00 – 25.00.** Author collection.

Beautiful blue set of Zoe Coste Design clip-on earrings. The glass stones have an AB finish to the back of them making light appear inside the stones. Both earrings are signed, differently. One is signed "Zoe Coste Design" on the back of the earring clip; the other is signed "Zoe Coste Made in France" on a signature plaque on the top back of the earring. The large stones are prong set. 1⅝" tall. **$65.00 – 75.00.** Author collection.

Amber and topaz clip-on earrings. The topaz pear stones are unfoiled and open backed. The earrings are 1". **$20.00 – 30.00.** Author collection.

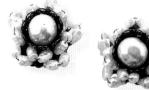

Faux pearl earrings with wired-on pearls surrounding a large baroque pearl. 1⅜" in diameter. **$65.00 – 75.00.** Barbara Wood collection.

These flirty earrings from the 1970s feature rhinestone beads and dangle nearly 4". They are for pierced ears. **$75.00 – 85.00.** Barbara Wood collection.

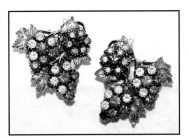

These bright and beautiful earrings are a grape design with grape clusters and leaves. They are unsigned, from the 1950s, and 1⅞" tall. **$50.00 – 60.00.** Barbara Wood collection.

These earrings look like the Weiss thermoplastic ones set with embedded rhinestones. They are pink, unsigned, and measure 1⅛" x 1". **$65.00 – 75.00.** Barbara Wood collection.

One of these earrings is signed with something that looks like s.s.m. Capade by Joni. They are colorful collage work with a glass center ball surrounded by bright rhinestones. 1½" in diameter. **$75.00 – 95.00.** Barbara Wood collection.

These faux pearl earrings recall the design of Miriam Haskell but a close look reveals that the tiny seed pearls are glued and not wired. They dangle to a length of 3¼". **$75.00 – 85.00.** Barbara Wood collection.

Bold use of red stones highlight these Vrba earrings, accented with clear stones. 1⅝" x 1". **$55.00 – 65.00.** Barbara Wood collection.

Faux pearl earrings by Larry Vrba. 2" x 1⅜". **$65.00 – 75.00.** Barbara Wood collection.

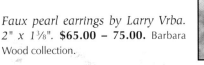

Rings and Things

This is quite a rare find, a DuJay ring in sterling. There is a large green glass center stone surrounded by clear rhinestones. **$275.00 – 350.00.** Carol Bell Treasures-In-Time collection.

Hobé ring with large rainbow stone, size 7. **$95.00 – 115.00.** Carol Bell Treasures-In-Time collection.

Panetta ring with turquoise colored stones, size 6. **$55.00 – 65.00.** Carol Bell Treasures-In-Time collection.

Kenneth Lane bold ring with oversize Lucite stone, adjustable. **$70.00 – 75.00.** Carol Bell Treasures-In-Time collection.

Hollycraft sapphire blue ring signed "Hollycraft 1952." **$75.00 – 80.00.** Carol Bell Treasures-In-Time collection.

Hollycraft adjustable ring in purples, light and dark. **$80.00 – 85.00.** Carol Bell Treasures-In-Time collection.

Unmarked adjustable clear rhinestone ring accented with blue baguettes. **$125.00 – 135.00.** Carol Bell Treasures-In-Time collection.

Wouldn't these look good in your cuffed shirt? These Larry Vrba cufflinks have huge AB center stones and are 1⅛" in diameter. **$65.00 – 75.00.** Barbara Wood collection.

Pale grass green celluloid scarf holder with clear rhinestones. 1⅝" long. **$55.00 – 75.00.** Author collection.

Calvaire made this purse with the tiny beads that have been stitched on and none are missing. Inside is the "Made in France Especially for Calvaire New York" tag. A rare find. **$200.00 – 225.00.** Author collection.

Butterfly belt buckle with marcasites. 3¾" x 2". **$95.00 – 115.00.** Barbara Wood collection.

Contemporary Jewelry

This section features work by bead artist Annie Navetta, whose website can be found at www.AnnisOriginalArtJewelry.com. She is an amazing artist who works mostly with vintage beads, most of which are unused and previously unsold old store stock. Annie takes special orders, helping you to create the perfect jewels for the perfect outfit.

This section also includes designs by Ian St. Gielar for Stanley Hagler NYC. St. Gielar also creates amazing limited edition hand-beaded jewelry using vintage and contemporary findings and beads. His website features tons of beautiful photographs of his creations and can be found at www.stanleyhaglernyc.com.

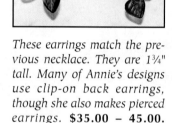

Here is a truly amazing necklace. Annie takes vintage beads and adds findings of all sorts and comes up with phenomenal creations, including many special orders. This necklace is loaded with milk glass beads and antiqued gold finish findings. Annie has taken flower-shaped beads and added smaller flower-shaped beads to create very dimensional flowers. The combination of the beads and the findings makes a joyful noise when the necklace is worn. The necklace is 22" long and has the "Anni" hang tag attached. **$200.00 – 250.00.** *Annie Navetta collection.*

Pinks and greens are used in this delicate beauty. Annie's work has been compared to that of Miriam Haskell, Larry Vrba, and Stanley Hagler. Russian gold-plated flowers, leaves, and base are all vintage Stanley Hagler stock; metal beads are vermeil. The necklace is 18" long with a pendant centerpiece of 3½". **$125.00 – 150.00.** *Annie Navetta collection.*

These earrings match the previous necklace. They are 1¾" tall. Many of Annie's designs use clip-on back earrings, though she also makes pierced earrings. **$35.00 – 45.00.** *Annie Navetta collection.*

This exquisite design by Annie features amethyst and lavender beads accented with greens and Czech glass flower beads. The necklace is 18" long with a pendant that is 2¼". Note the tiny butterfly perched at the top right of the pendant. **$150.00 – 175.00.** *Annie Navetta collection.*

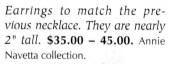

Earrings to match the previous necklace. They are nearly 2" tall. **$35.00 – 45.00.** *Annie Navetta collection.*

This aqua and turquoise colored bead necklace is an early Annie Navetta Original design. It features all vintage beads and findings. 17" long. **$100.00 – 125.00.** Barbara Wood collection.

This totally feminine Annie Navetta creation draws inspiration from the hand-beaded work of Miriam Haskell and Stanley Hagler. This green necklace has enameled findings, mother of pearl leaves, and Swarovski Margarita beads. Note the tiny tulip beads at the top left have seed beads tucked inside the flower's tip. The flower dangles at the bottom hang loosely to give the necklace movement. Necklace is 18" long with the "Anni" hang tag, with all vintage glass beads. **$150.00 – 175.00.** Annie Navetta collection.

Here is the matching bracelet, two strands, with a hand-wired centerpiece. The bracelet is 8" long. One of the best things about placing a special order for Annie's jewelry is that you get jewelry with a perfect fit. **$85.00 – 95.00.** Annie Navetta collection.

This Annie Navetta Original necklace with matching earrings features black vintage glass beads and findings. The necklace is 20" long and has the "Anni" hang tag attached. The earrings are 2½" long. All Annie Navetta jewelry is handmade. **$160.00 – 175.00.** Barbara Wood collection.

This masterful mix of coral and green glass beads features all the best of Annie's work, with the tiny tulip beads and combination flower beading. Russian gold-plated flowers, leaves, and base are all vintage Hagler stock. The back of the pin features a bale for wearing on a chain as a pendant. The pin is nearly 4" tall and beautifully handcrafted. The back of pin has "Anni" hang tag attached. The back is a vintage Hagler finding. **$125.00 – 165.00.** Annie Navetta collection.

This set was a special order from Annie Navetta. I wanted something in black and white that was long enough to wear outside of collared shirts. Annie's necklaces make that easy as the hook can be placed anywhere along the chain. This necklace has the perfect touch of white to accent the black. 25" long. **$275.00 – 325.00 for set.** Author collection.

I wanted a charm style bracelet to go with this set. This one makes perfect music. It is nearly 8" long but you need a little extra length when you wear this many beads.

Annie made me two different pairs of earrings to go with this set. One is all black beads and the other is black and white. Both hang 1½" long.

Close-up of pendant centerpiece.

This delightful necklace is an Annie Navetta original design. It is loaded with vintage fruit beads. Note the little lemons dangling from the bottom of the pendant, and the lemon and berry dangling on the clasp. This necklace also has apples, pears, and oranges. The necklace is 19" long and has an "Anni" hang tag attached. The pendant drop is 3½". **$150.00 – 175.00.** Annie Navetta collection.

Close-up of Anni signature hang tag.

This fruit pin matches the necklace and has a bale attached to allow you to wear it on a chain. 2¼" x 2⅛". $75.00 – 95.00. Annie Navetta collection.

I don't even have the words to tell you how fantastic this expansion bracelet is, you just have to believe me. It is loaded with vintage beads and tons of fruit beads, and even some beads that look like green corn. Annie does an amazing job. This bracelet is over 1½" wide. $175.00 – 200.00. Annie Navetta collection.

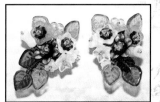

Lovely little earrings with green flowers. These pierced earrings are 1⅝" tall. $35.00 – 45.00. Annie Navetta collection.

This remarkable necklace uses amethyst glass beads, faceted glass stones, and rhinestone rondelles. It is stunning. The necklace is 18" long, the pendant drops are 2½" long, and the matching earrings are 2¾" long. $125.00 – 145.00. Annie Navetta collection.

This astonishing expansion bracelet is my favorite Annie Navetta design. It is covered with glorious beads and even rare rhinestone head pins. The occasional little pink fruit bead is also presented. I particularly love the flowers made from two different colored flower beads. These bracelets are heavy but extremely comfortable to wear. This one is over 1½" wide. $175.00 – 225.00. Author collection.

Before you pick up this hinged cuff bracelet and check for a mark, you will think it is a Miriam Haskell design. It evokes all the best design elements of Haskell but it is a Stanley Hagler Ian St. Gielar design. The hand-wired beads go all the way around the back and sides of the bracelet. This is an exceptional bracelet. $450.00 – 500.00. Ian St. Gielar collection.

Side view of bracelet.

157

This necklace is one of the most spectacular I have ever had the honor and fortune to hold in my hands. It is a Stanley Hagler Ian St. Gielar design in shades of green. The center piece is 7" wide and the middle one hangs almost 5½" long. The back has two signature plaques on it, "Stanley Hagler NYC" and "Ian St. Gieler." Overall length is 17" with a 3" extension. The handwork on this one-of-a-kind necklace is extraordinary. **$850.00 – 1,000.00.** Author collection.

Close-up view of side pendants.

This utterly fantastic pearl necklace is not for the faint of heart. It is a heavy faux pearl collar with two pendant attachments with pins on the back to stay where you place them. Each side pendant is covered with hand-wired seed pearls, beads, and rhinestones. Each is 2¼" x 2¾". Each end of the collar has 4" pearl drops. With this necklace you are beautiful coming and going. **$850.00 – 1,000.00.** Ian St. Gielar collection.

This beautiful coffee with cream faux baroque pearl collar has a heart-shaped center piece of AB rhinestones. The necklace is 14" long with a 4" extension. **$350.00 – 400.00.** Ian St. Gielar collection.

This necklace features a dragonfly flitting among the flower blossoms. This hand-wired beauty has chryophrase green beads. The pendant is 3⅝" x 3¾" and the necklace is 17" long with a 3" extension. The back of the pendant has both Hagler and St. Gielar signature plaques. **$400.00 – 450.00.** Ian St. Gielar collection.

This butterfly necklace gets you ready for Mardi Gras in a hurry. A huge carved green glass pendant peeks from the bottom of the centerpiece. The pendant is 4" x 4". The three-strand necklace is 17½" long with a 3" extension. **$400.00 – 450.00.** Ian St. Gielar collection.

This magnificent 5" pin is the creation of Ian St. Gieler and Stanley Hagler N.Y.C. It truly is a work of art. This oversize brooch features the hand beading Hagler designs are famous for along with the inspiration of a mother and baby monkey resting in the center. They appear to be sitting in the middle of a colorful rain forest with giant banana leaves gracefully flowing overhead and underneath. Photographs could not capture its beauty. This brooch has both the Stanley Hagler and Ian St. Gieler plaques applied to the back. **$500.00 – 600.00.** Author collection.

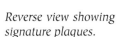

Reverse view showing signature plaques.

This pin is perfectly beautiful to wear year round but it is especially appropriate to wear during the Christmas holidays. It is a gorgeous green and red with purple accents. The pin is 3¾" x 3" and has both Hagler and St. Gielar signature plaques on the back. **$250.00 – 300.00.** Author collection.

Here is a flower garden pin in full bloom. It has flowers of all colors, including a lovely rose. It is all hand-wired. The pin has both Hagler and St. Gieler signature plaques on the back. It is 3¾" x 3¼". **$250.00 – 300.00.** Ian St. Gielar collection.

This beautiful coral beaded pin from Ian St. Gielar features amazing handwork. It is 4" wide by 4¼" tall and signed "Ian St. Gielar." **$450.00 – 500.00.** Ian St. Gielar collection.

This is the most beautifully designed butterfly pin I have ever seen. Like most of the wonderful Hagler St. Gielar designs it is large and bold. Note the hand-wired antennas. The butterfly is nearly 5" wide and is 3¾" tall, not including antenna. It has both signature plaques on the back. **$150.00 – 200.00.** Ian St. Gielar collection.

There is a touch of nature in this lovely pink seashell pin and earrings that are an Ian St. Gielar for Stanley Hagler design. Beads are captured in oversized bead caps between sliced seashells, and they surround hand-wired flowers. The pin is 3" in diameter and the earrings are 1½" in diameter. **$400.00 – 450.00.** Author collection.

A lovely basket of flowers in pastel colors, this pin has the Stanley Hagler NYC plaque on the back. It is 3" wide and 2⅞" tall. **$125.00 – 150.00.** Ian St. Gielar collection.

Here is a departure from the flamboyant beaded Hagler designs. This stick pin with matching earrings in gold-tone is also hand-wired with a floral design. The stick pin is 4" long and the earrings are 1" tall. **$125.00 – 150.00.** Ian St. Gielar collection.

This lovely gold-tone pin with clear rhinestone accents has the Stanley Hagler NYC plaque on the back. It is 2¾" x 3". **$100.00 – 125.00.** Ian St. Gielar collection.

These rhinestone cuff links for your fanciest shirts were made by Stanley Hagler NYC. Each cuff is 1½" in diameter and only one has the signature plaque. **$100.00 – 125.00.** Ian St. Gielar collection.

This chatelaine has lovely flower pins separated by chains with faux pearls. The pins are 1" and 1¼" and the chain is 4" long. The pin on the right has Hagler signature plaque on the back. **$100.00 – 150.00.** Ian St. Gielar collection.

These are hand-wired green and pale pink flower earrings by Stanley Hagler NYC. They are 1½" in diameter. **$75.00 – 100.00.** Ian St. Gielar collection.

These hand-wired earrings have orange accents. They are 1⅛" in diameter and are signed "Stanley Hagler NYC." **$75.00 – 100.00.** Ian St. Gielar collection.

Selling Your Jewelry

One of the best places to sell your old costume jewelry is at an online auction. There are several things you need to be aware of before you list your items. Buy a magnifying glass *before* you start listing jewelry so that you can look at it up close. Marks are hidden sometimes on the sides of bracelets, or on the spring ring or even the circular clasp. Countess Cissy Zoltowska marked some of her brooches on the long thin pin itself, even Trifari marked a few on the pin. You will overlook these very important marks if you don't give the jewelry a good once-over. Most importantly, *do not split up sets*. You will realize much higher profits by keeping these together. Trust me on this.

Research: Do your research first. If you are listing jewelry online, then you have the perfect venue for research. Get into the jewelry and watches category and look around for the item you are thinking of listing. Be sure to check completed auctions. You may be surprised at what some people will pay. Take the Napier pink glass elephant bracelet. I recently saw it offered at auction with only one of the elephants being sold, no bracelet. The seller took the other ones off of the bracelet, and sold the one elephant with four matching beads for $6.99. Had they done some research, they would have discovered that collectors do want a bracelet with perfect elephants, but they also realize that the elephants are made of glass and you can't expect them to have no damage, just from normal wearing. The bracelet with the elephants attached would probably have brought a final bid of more than $100.00, maybe as much as $200.00 with perfect elephants. Not all broken jewelry can make this claim, so you have to take a few minutes to do some research. And fortunately, the seller offered the buyer all of the parts of the bracelet, so I was able to restore it to its original beauty.

Photos: You should take the very best photographs of the jewelry that you can, and make sure to take front and back photos. Get close-ups of any marks that you see. If you do not have a camera that can take great photos of jewelry, you can simply use a scanner. Jewelry items placed right on top of the bed of the scanner reproduce beautifully. You may have to tweak the color on some items, but if you can't get it just right, state in the description that the color is "more" of whatever is most appropriate. Under no circumstances should you ever show your jewelry being worn by anyone, unless it is an ad with a movie star wearing the jewelry.

Pricing: Look around at the different categories in the section where you are going to list the jewelry. Be as truthful as you can, the item itself will verify the truth. Don't put an unsigned piece of jewelry in the signed category; buyers will skip off as fast as possible because they view you as untruthful. Or even worse, the buyer may demand a refund because there is no mark or signature. This only costs you more time and money in the long run, because you will have to refund fees, ask the online auction for refunds, and then relist and have to reship. Your time is valuable too, make it right the first time and have a very happy buyer.

Description: Be completely honest about the condition of the jewelry and any marks. Those who buy regularly know all the tricks a seller can use to get them to look at their auctions, and most of the time it does not work. The buyer knows what they want and what they are looking at, and honesty is always the best policy. Give the best description you can of the jewelry, including sizes, colors, and condition. You don't have to get flowery, just do the best you can. And be careful. Most buyers laugh at sellers who sell "necklesses" and "chockers" instead of necklaces and chokers. Besides, if you have a "neckless" to sell, doesn't that refer to "the absence of a neck?" Use your word processing program to type your description and let it check your spelling. You can also just type it in ahead of time and then cut and paste into the auction description area. This is especially important when you are selling a signed piece of jewelry and you "guess" at it when you enter the signature. A "Channel" bracelet might get you a bid of $20.00, but a "Chanel" will bring hundreds, maybe even thousands. Above all, do not be cute or creative when you are writing the title for the auction. You may think that listing a "Bobble Bracelet" is a cute way to attract attention, but with so many listings, collectors don't physically have time to look at each one, and if they want a Napier black and white art glass bead charm bracelet, and are willing to pay more than $50.00 for it. Your "Bobble Bracelet" is not going to attract the buyers you want and will sell for less than ten dollars. To me!

Props: Sometimes you may need to use some type of prop in your photographs to get the jewelry shown properly. Under no circumstances should you hold the jewelry in your hand or show a ring or bracelet being worn on someone's hand, most especially a man's hand. If the only way you know how to take a photo of a ring is by holding it or wearing it, then cover your hand with a tissue or paper towel or some type of plain fabric. Lovely rhinestone rings do not sell when they are being worn on the very hairy fingers of a man.

Backgrounds: Always use the plainest background you can find, unless you are a professional photographer. White tissue or paper towels may seem silly to use, but you want the buyers to see the jewelry, not what is behind it. Busy fabrics remove definition from the jewelry and may cause you to get a much smaller price for it.

Packing: Most importantly do not wrap the jewelry itself in packing tape. Period. When buyers try to remove the jewelry, most of the time it is going to be damaged and you are going to have to give a refund. Even the most careful person might scratch it when they are trying to remove the mummified jewelry. You are not saving yourself any money by trying to recycle flimsy boxes or bubble wrap envelopes when shipping jewelry. This may work perfectly for other items but trust me; with jewelry, it will catch up with you in the end. Do you realize that the post office uses machines to cancel packages? That means the little pin you wrapped in leftover Christmas tissue and stuck in a bubble wrap envelope will be smashed through the machine to be cancelled. Too many packages go through the post office every day, and just because you thoughtfully write "Fragile — Hand Stamp Please" does not mean that your package will receive special handling, as much as you and the post office hope otherwise. Too many packages go through too fast and the chance of yours being caught and hand cancelled is slim. Don't try to recycle every old box you come in contact with when shipping jewelry. The post office gives away boxes, free, and in the long run, this will pay off better for you. Making a couple extra dollars on shipping may seem like a good idea, but it is not. I will explain more about this later.

Shipping and handling: I use the Priority Mail boxes that are flat and fold up. First I wrap the jewelry in fresh tissue paper. Next I put the wrapped jewelry inside a sandwich bag that zips shut. This is in case the package for some reason becomes wet. It happens, believe me. A copy of the invoice with the buyer's name and address is folded up inside the sandwich bag. If the bag somehow separates from the box, the post office can still deliver it to the right person. I then tape the bag itself to the inside of the Priority Mail box. No shaking around inside, no noise. I seal the box, address, it and then I add extra tape. The extra tape goes on either side where the slots slide in, and on the ends of both sides. I have received packages before where they were "stepped" on and the jewelry slid right out of the box. If one of the Priority Mail boxes gets squished in transit in any way and an opening appears at one of the junctures listed above, the jewelry slips away, and somebody is out some money. And that somebody will usually be you.

Addressing: I received a package this year that looked like a cat had written my name and address on it. Not one single word was legible. The reason, the only reason, it arrived at my house was because I always use the zip code-plus four on my return address. It was the only thing the postal carrier could read, but it was exactly enough to get the package to me. If you don't use your computer to print off an address label, and you end up writing it by hand, always print the name and address, don't write in cursive. Also consider using a permanent marker to write the address with, as it will remain legible and visible even if it gets wet. If you are shipping an item that is over $100.00, and the buyer didn't tell you their zip code-plus four, you can go online to any number of sites and get the extra four digits easily. Many of the sites that give directions also show you the extra four when you enter the address. I always look these up when I am shipping books; I honestly believe it gets your mail where it is going quicker.

Insurance: I always make insurance mandatory on any item of jewelry that I sell. Tell the buyer right up front in the description that insurance is required, and then list the amounts. Insurance is always the same amount; it doesn't fluctuate. There is a tiny chart at the post office website or available from your post office that states the amounts of insurance in $100.00 increments. Put it in your shipping requirements and stick to it. However, some people who pay a few dollars for a piece of jewelry do not want to pay the extra $5.00 or $6.00 to have it shipped. Fine, you pay the insurance for your peace of mind, because if it gets lost, you file the claim and get the money back. Also, there is something called Delivery Confirmation that costs less than .50 cents. You will be doing yourself another inexpensive favor if you do this to cover yourself. Just add $1.00 to the lowest price you will accept for the item, the starting price, and you won't be out of pocket for the expense.

Reputation and feedback: Don't think that because you are one of millions online selling that no one knows who you are or cares about you as a seller. There are jewelry clubs all over the world who happily share info about sellers whom they have had problems with, even if that problem was resolved. You would be amazed how quickly hundreds or even thousands of the very buyers you want will report your poor treatment of them. Being online made us more of a small community than ever. And while feedback is important, don't worry if you end up with one or two bad reports. Sometimes it is impossible to please a buyer, no matter what you do. But be aware, if you get too many bad feedbacks, you could lose your selling privileges.

Singles and lots: I am constantly amazed that sellers will list a plain undesirable piece of jewelry by itself with a high starting price, or worse, a starting price of one cent. Your fees will be much higher than this because you won't sell the item. Consider combining all of the lower end jewelry you have for sale, you will be much happier with the results and the money you save yourself.

Vintage Ads

A great many dealers and collectors have continued to seek vintage ads showing costume jewelry. Many websites now have pages showing the ads they have collected. A few even show the actual jewelry that is pictured in the ad. I love these old ads and continue to collect them. I hope you enjoy the ones I have selected to share with you.

Hattie Carnegie, 1946, *Harper's Bazaar.*

JEWELS OF TANJORE, like all Jewels by Trifari, are
such exquisite fashion pieces they are
usually thought to be real jewels.

Jewels by
TRIFARI
Designs patented

Suit by Pauline Trigère
Furs by Esther Dorothy
Photo by Rawlings

Trifari Jewels of Tanjore, 1946, *Harper's Bazaar.*

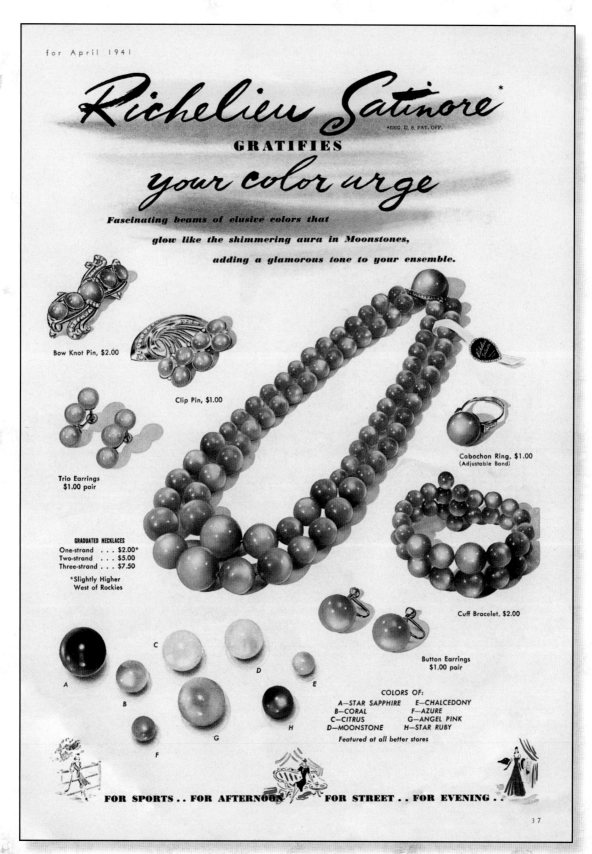

Richelieu Satinore, 1941, *Mademoiselle*.

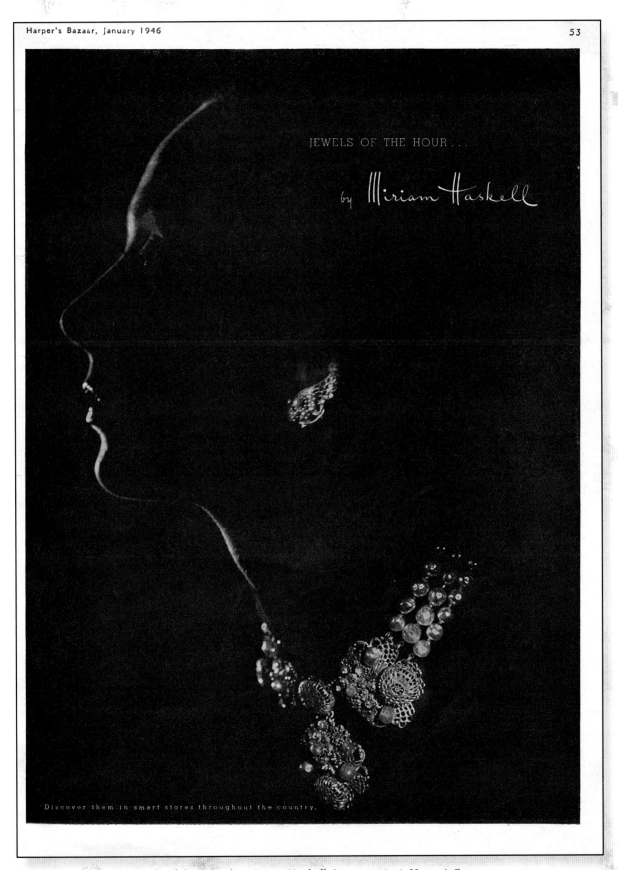

Jewels of the Hour by Miriam Haskell, January 1946, *Harper's Bazaar.*

JEWELS *Miriam Haskell*

DISCOVER THEM IN SMART STORES THROUGHOUT THE COUNTRY. MIRIAM HASKELL, 392 FIFTH AVENUE, NEW YORK, N.Y.

Jewels Miriam Haskell, 1949, *Vogue (incorporating Vanity Fair)*.

1948

JEWELS *Miriam Haskell*

392 FIFTH AVENUE. NEW YORK, N. Y.

Jewels Miriam Haskell, February 14, 1948, *Vogue.*

by Miriam Haskell

DISCOVER THEM IN SMART STORES THROUGHOUT THE COUNTRY. MIRIAM HASKELL, 392 FIFTH AVENUE, NEW YORK, N.Y.

By Miriam Haskell, 1947, *Vogue.*

ETOILE...
breath-taking magnificence
in a startlingly beautiful
jewel series by Trifari!
Nuggets of pure light caught
amidst the rainbowing facets
of fabulous fake gems!
Sheer wizardry for fashion's
elegant simplicity!

...obviously by TRIFARI

From 7.50 to 25.00, plus tax.
Earrings to match. Jewelry designs
copyrighted by Trifari.

Etoile obviously by Trifari, 1959, *Vogue*.

Pardon me, but there's a ladybug on your collar

a penguin on your scarf

a parrot on your shoulder

and a flock of birds on your lapel

a strawberry on your belt

a row of flowers on your sleeve

a starfish on your pocket

and your flair for fashion is showing.

Jewels by TRIFARI®

EACH PIN ABOUT $5   JEWELRY DESIGNS COPYRIGHTED: TRIFARI, KRUSSMAN AND FISHEL, INC.

Pardon me, but there's a ladybug on your collar…, Trifari, 1968, *Vogue.*

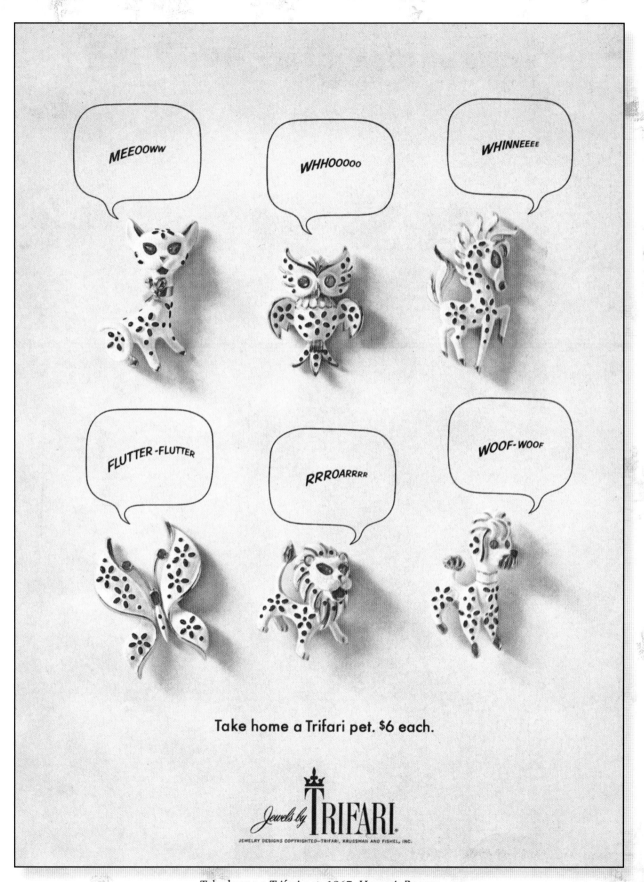

Take home a Trifari pet, 1967, *Harper's Bazaar.*

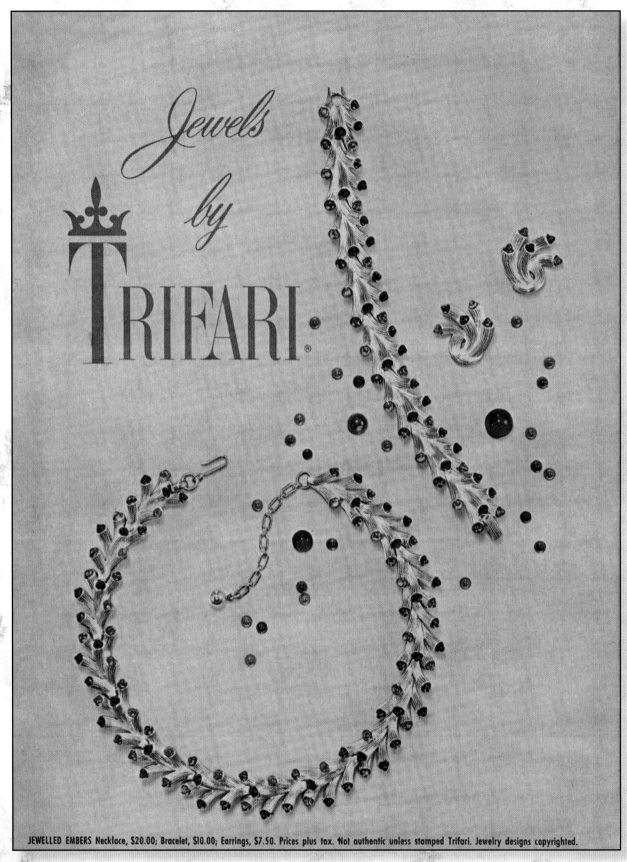

JEWELLED EMBERS Necklace, $20.00; Bracelet, $10.00; Earrings, $7.50. Prices plus tax. Not authentic unless stamped Trifari. Jewelry designs copyrighted.

Jewelled Embers by Trifari, 1955, *Vogue*.

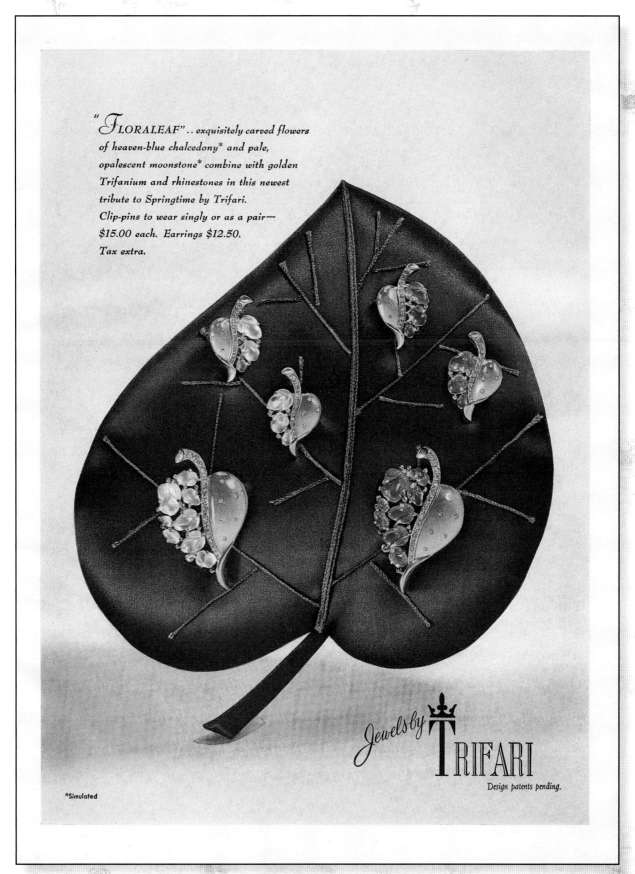

"FLORALEAF".. exquisitely carved flowers
of heaven-blue chalcedony* and pale,
opalescent moonstone* combine with golden
Trifanium and rhinestones in this newest
tribute to Springtime by Trifari.
Clip-pins to wear singly or as a pair—
$15.00 each. Earrings $12.50.
Tax extra.

*Simulated

Jewels by TRIFARI

Design patents pending.

Floraleaf by Trifari, 1948, Vogue.

Vintage Ads

Schiaparelli jewelry Bonwit Teller, 1938, *Harper's Bazaar.*

Champagne Morning Schiaparelli Jewels, 1957, *Vogue*.

*J*ewelled lace, opposite page, in a collar of rhinestones shimmering with false turquoise drop-lets—this necklace shape is important, a graceful pendant collar tapered toward the clasp, to wear either with a covered-up satin dress or theatre suit, or with a long bare evening dress. The hat, a peacock-green beaded and rhinestoned turban, swathed in veiling, is too much of a dazzler in its own right to get along in real life with much jewellery; by Sally Victor. The make-up with all this brilliant fakery should be a clear warm natural counterpoint; like the one on this page, for instance; by Estée Lauder. Necklace, by Scaasi, about $90* at Bonwit Teller; Harzfeld's; Frederick & Nelson. This page, top row: Sea-flower pin, its petals delicate sprays of twisted gilt, to bloom at night amid ropes of pearls, or on a suit during the day. Pin by Monet, $10* at Saks Fifth Avenue; Hutzler's. Bogus pavé pearls dangling like grapes from gilt and rhinestones whorls, eloquent enough to star alone without a necklace. These earrings by Vendôme, about $10*, at Altman's; Meier & Frank. Snowflake of rhinestones hung with a pseudo pearl—as some of the freshest-looking pins are this season. By Richelieu, $10*, at Henri Bendel; Hutzler's. Entwined glitter, one three-strand necklace of baroque pseudo pearls mixed with gilt and rhinestone beads, and a four-strand necklace of baroque pseudo pearls alternated with cut glass balls. Both necklaces by Valjean, the three strand one, $7.50*; four strands $10*, at Bloomingdale's. Rhinestone ribbon bowed and looped through a fake emerald centre, dangling another bogus emerald by a rhinestone thread—a wonderful way to tie up a bare little black crêpe or champagne-and-lemon brocade evening suit. Pin by Joseph Mazer, about $40*, at Bonwit Teller. Second row: Coiled crescent moon of rhinestones that is rayed with fake pearls—just one of the places it looks dashing is pinned to the side of a gold lamé or velvet beret. Pin by Schreiner, about $36*, at Lord & Taylor; Frederick & Nelson. Gilt ribbon bracelet textured like grosgrain and edged in rhinestones, by Kramer about $5* at Lord & Taylor; Burdine's. Sprays of gilt dusted with rhinestones, a pair of the smaller earrings to balance a great pendant jewelled collar or excesses of fake pearls. These earrings by Bergère, about $10*, at Bonwit Teller; Gus Mayer.

*PLUS TAX

HORST

101

More Late-Day Glitter, *Vogue.*

Red construction page, mixed jewels, 1952, *Vogue*.

Devastating Amethyst, Coro Craft, 1944, *Vogue*.

Basic
necessity
for Basic
Black

Eisenberg Ice

Subtle splendor…ablaze
with dramatic brilliance against starkest black—and
gem-set like the world's finest jewels.
Pins $10 to $25, Earrings $15, Necklace $25, Bracelet $45.
Prices plus tax.

Eisenberg Jewelry, 22 West Madison Street, Chicago
14 East 38th Street, New York

Authentic only when trademarked Eisenberg. Eisenberg designs copyrighted

Basic necessity for Basic Black, Eisenberg Ice, 1960, *Vogue.*

DRESSMAKERS • JEWELERS • PERFUMERS • EISENBERG & SONS,   MERCHANDISE MART, CHICAGO

Pink ad for Eisenberg, 1947, *Vogue*.

Pink ad for Eisenberg, 1947, *Vogue*.

Coro, White 'n Hue, 1959, *Life.*

Love Birds by Coro, 1954, *Vogue.*

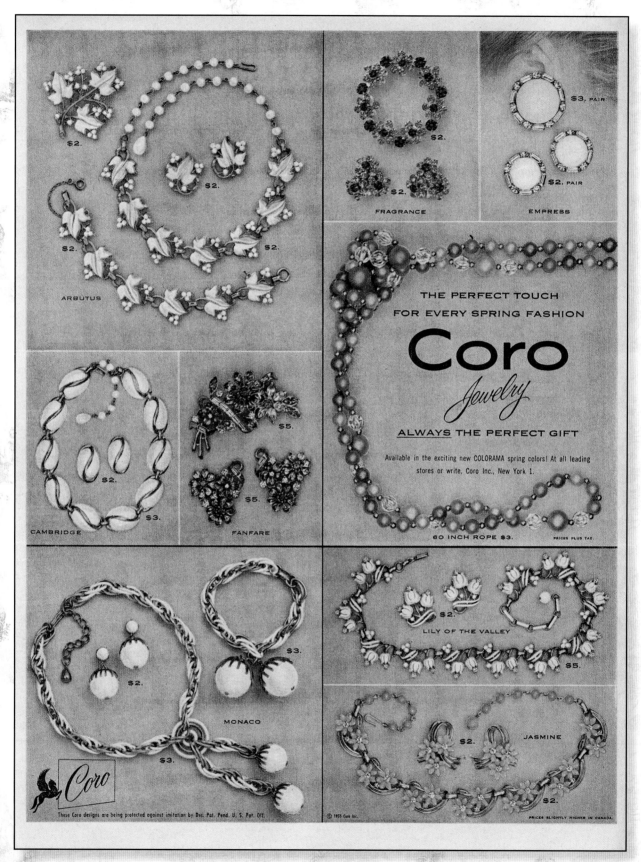

The Perfect Touch by Coro Jewelry, 1955, *Life*.

Across top: "Meteor" set — Earrings **$7.50**, Necklace **$10**, Bracelet **$12.50.** Second row: "Snowflake" pin **$7.50**, (smaller size **$4**), Earrings **$5** — Rhinestone Leaf **$20.** Third row: Book Locket Bracelet **$5**, "Scheherazade" Pendant Necklace **$20**, "Scheherazade" Clip Pin **$25**, Pendant Earrings **$15.** Fourth Row: "Golden Twist" Necklace **$10**, Earrings **$5**, (matching bracelet **$6**). Tax extra.

This Christmas…, Jewels by Trifari, 1949, *Harper's Bazaar.*

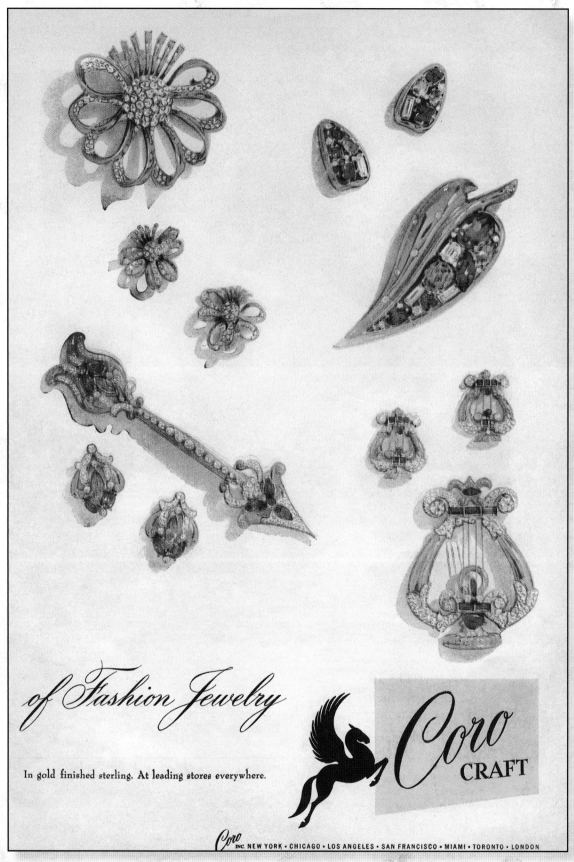

of Fashion Jewelry

In gold finished sterling. At leading stores everywhere.

Coro
CRAFT

Coro INC. NEW YORK · CHICAGO · LOS ANGELES · SAN FRANCISCO · MIAMI · TORONTO · LONDON

Of Fashion Jewelry, Coro Craft, 1946, *Vogue*.

A Collection of Sparkling Coro Craft Splendor…, 1946, *Vogue*.

Costume Jewelry Internet Websites

There is now a tremendous amount of websites offering vintage costume jewelry. Some of the very best offer more than just jewelry for sale, many offer free educational tools. Volume one offered 35 websites, and this chapter continues with completely different websites. In addition to the ones listed, you can find many more vintage costume jewelry sites at larger "stores" such as Tias.com and RubyLane.com. These sites are both important, but their individual sites are too numerous to mention. They are easy to navigate when you are ready to "shop" their "stores."

Each website was given the same questionnaire, which follows. Many of these website owners belong to these groups which will be abbreviated in the listing, the Vintage Fashion & Costume Jewelry club is listed as VFCJ, Jewelcollect is listed as JC, and JewelryRing is listed as JR. Information about these groups follows the websites listing for those wishing to join or to obtain additional information. Use this section also if you are trying to sell some jewelry. Each site lists what they are actively seeking to aid your search for a buyer for your jewelry.

Many of the sites listed below have weekly or monthly newsletters that are free. Visit each site and sign up for those you are interested in, and get advance notice of sales and updates.

Because of the economic times, some of these long term sites may have disappeared by the time the book has been published. I apologize for any confusion this may cause.

The Questionnaire:

Date your site started.
Owners names.
What exactly do you carry?
What do you consider to be your specialty?
Is there any costume jewelry you are actively seeking?
Would you like sellers to contact you; if so, how?
Does your site have a buyer's wish list?
Do you belong to any professional organizations?
Do you do appraisals?

Is there any additional information you would like included? Please use this section to "chat" with your future buyers to either tell them about yourself or what makes you or your website of special interest to them.

Bitz of Glitz
Delores and William Benedict
www.bitzofglitz.com
Est. 2002

Offering: vintage and contemporary jewelry and vintage compacts

Specialty: unsigned vintage jewelry

Seeking: quality signed vintage jewelry at a reasonable price

Contact: my phone number is on website

Organizations: VFCJ and JC

No appraisals.

Comments: My husband and I are a team and our goal is to have a great selection of vintage costume jewelry at reasonable prices. Customer service is first on our list.

The Lush Life Antiques
Erik Yang
www.thelushlifeantiques.com
Est. 2003

Offering: I offer an eclectic mix of jewelry from antique to contemporary. Each piece is carefully hand selected for its design, construction, quality, or wearability.

Specialty: I try to focus on statement pieces. Whether it's a bracelet, necklace, or earrings, I like for the pieces to stand alone on their own merit. I strive to find the rare and hard to find. My interests are primarily European and couture jewelry.

Seeking: I'm always buying. I'm happy to look at anything available for sale.

Contact: thelushlife@mindspring.com

Organizations: VFCJ, JR, and JC.

No appraisals.

Pretty Snazzy
Stefanie and David Brawner
www.prettysnazzy.com
Est. 2002

Offering: Vintage jewelry, loose Swarovski, Czech & German rhinestones, imitation & genuine pearls, marcasites, cabochons, rhinestone repair kits, glue, and other miscellaneous stones for jewelry repair and design

Specialty: Rhinestones — especially Swarovski

Seeking: Costume jewelry that needs repair, TLC

Contact: sales@prettysnazzy.net

Organizations: VFCJ, JC, JR, International Jewelry Designers' Guild

No appraisals.

Comments: We have a huge selection of stones including thousands of different styles, colors, shapes, and sizes of rhinestones both new and vintage. Also available online are complete instructions to help you do your own repairs. Professional stone replacement is also available for a reasonable fee. Please e-mail for information.

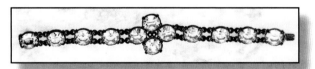

Edgewater Vintage Jewels
Jan Cox
www.EdgewaterVintageJewels.com
Est. 2006

Offering: Vintage costume jewelry, vintage stickpins, vintage glassware, silver and porcelain collectibles

Specialty: Florenza jewelry, vintage stickpins

Seeking: Interested in early Trifari and Hobé pieces or sets, always looking for large glitzy flower brooches from the Art Deco through Retro period, and for Victorian/Edwardian topaz glass jewelry of all kinds

Contact: Bunnyflowerlady@aol.com

Organizations: VFCJ, JC, JR, Discovering Juliana Jewelry

No appraisals.

Comments: I have been collecting costume jewelry for over 25 years and selling on the Internet for five years. We do offer a lay-away plan and will be happy to "hold" items for a reasonable period of time. Of special interest is my Florenza archive (picture library) for reference/research with pictures of the front and back of over 500 signed and unsigned items. Unsigned items have been verified by my good friend, Mr. Larry Kasoff, son of Dan Kasoff, founder of Florenza.

Vintage Jewelry Online
Shelley Osborne
www.vintagejewelryonline.com
Est. 2005

Offering: Vintage Jewelry Online specializes in vintage, upscale costume and estate jewelry including designer signed, unsigned collectible jewelry, Bakelite of all eras and fine gold and sterling.

Specialty: Signed costume pieces and fine gold items from the Victorian and Edwardian eras as well as Bakelite

Seeking: High end signed pieces — 40s Trifari, Dior, Chanel, Pennino, rare Bakelite figural or fruit necklaces, apple juice Bakelite bracelets, celluloid rhinestone bracelets, and Georg Jensen

Contact: shelley@vintagejewelryonline.com

Buyer's wish list offered.

Organizations: JC, Jewelry Talk Club, and VFCJ

Appraisals available.

Comments: In 1987 I went from being a collector to a seller, turning my love of jewelry into a business devoted to buying vintage and estate jewelry and selling them in three antiques stores in New Hampshire. Vintage Jewelry Online.com grew out of my brick and mortar business as a way to bring my collection to lovers of extraordinary jewelry and accessories across the globe. Although I am one of the largest sellers of Bakelite and plastic jewelry in this area, I am known for my hard-to-find signed pieces and great taste for unsigned pieces that have "the look." I have a reputation for quality and service and look forward to finding you items you will love.

Yesterdays Jewels
Linda Heberling
www.yesterdaysjewels.com
www.tias.com/stores/yesterdaysjewels
Est. 2003

Offering: I carry a wide variety of jewelry including vintage costume, antique jewelry, Art Deco, Art Nouveau, Victorian, Bakelite, Lucite, and vintage plastic jewelry, figurals, estate and fine jewelry, contemporary and artisan jewelry, as well as a broad range of collectibles and antiques. I have over 3,000 items between my two shops at this time...and counting!

Specialty: My specialty is signed costume jewelry from the 40s through the 80s.

Seeking: I always have my eye open for old enameled or unusual Coro pieces, bold Art Deco bracelets, large clear rhinestone brooches, elegant Victorian bar pins, and figurals.

Contact: jewels@yesterdaysjewels.com

Buyer's wish list offered.

Organizations: JC

No appraisals but I often provide specific information or point people in the right direction to assist them in their own research.

Comments: Collectors may want to check our article section. We currently have two articles that are accessed frequently:
1) Vintage Jewelry Values — a comprehensive overview of how jewelry is assessed and priced that is also valuable for collectors as they buy jewelry and build their collection, and
2) About Our Single Earrings — a short article that shares a few ways that single earrings can be used. Also, we always have a large number of currently unlisted single earrings (signed and unsigned) and always welcome e-mails from people looking to replace a favorite lost earring. We offer a generous "Returning Customer Discount" that brings customers back again and again.

Granny's Jewelry Box
Pat Hamm
www.grannysjewelrybox.com
Est. 1997

Offering: I carry mostly jewelry, some fine and but mostly costume (vintage to contemporary). I also carry ladies small accessories, purses and hats will be coming soon.

Specialty: I specialize in designer rhinestone jewelry.

Customers can reach me live online to talk about jewelry.

Contact: grjewlbx@verizon.net

Organizations: VFCJ, JC, and JR.

No appraisals.

Comments: Granny's Jewelry Box is the first vintage jewelry site to give website viewers a virtual peek at their entire inventory and make it searchable by designer, type of jewelry (ie. bracelet, necklace, etc.), price range, or any combination thereof. This is in addition to the traditional website.

Sassy Classics Vintage Jewelry, Antique Jewelry, and Estate Jewelry
Sandy Parke aka "Sassy"
www.sassyclassics.com
Est. 2000

Offering: High end antique and vintage costume necklaces and antique fine estate jewelry including ladies' antique watches, rings, and cameos

Specialty: Victorian necklaces, both fine and costume, from the 1860s to 1890s and Miriam Haskell necklaces

Seeking: Authentic colorful early Miriam Haskell necklaces

Contact: If you have Miriam Haskell chokers or necklaces e-mail sassy@sassyclassics.com

No appraisals.

Comments: I love the unusual and rare colorful antique jewelry, especially the jewelry from the 1800s and early 1900s. Chokers, bracelets, and ladies' unique wrist watches are my passion.

Let's Get Vintage
Marie Galterio
www.letsgetvintage.com

Offering: I specialize in larger-size rhinestone/crystal vintage costume jewelry pieces that make a definitive fashion statement. Sherman jewelry from Canada is a particular favorite.

Seeking: I am looking for Trifari, Sherman, Stanley Hagler, Swarovski, and Ciner vintage jewelry. I also buy vintage costume pieces from other designers that are comparable to items on my website. They must be in excellent to mint condition.

Contact: mrgvintage@optonline.net

Organizations: JC

No appraisals.

Comments: I offer quality vintage costume jewelry. Here you will find beautiful signed and unsigned pieces from designers such as Marcel Boucher, Alice Caviness, Ciner, Jomaz, Stanley Hagler, Sherman, and Trifari, to name just a few. When you visit my website you'll find the jewelry offered is in excellent to mint condition. As a customer or prospective customer, you'll receive the friendly, personalized service that I would expect to receive as well as frequent e-mail updates on the status of purchases made. I love the jewelry I present and want my customers to be happy and satisfied with their purchases. It brings me great joy to know that the careful choices I've made in selecting my jewelry have been recognized and appreciated. I believe you will enjoy my website, so please do stop by, enjoy viewing the beautiful jewelry you'll find in the various categories, check my Feedback page, and do drop me a note with any questions you may have. I look forward to meeting you!

A Fantasy of Jewels
Louise Champion
www.afantasyofjewels.completewebpages.com
Est. 2004

Offering: I carry vintage costume jewelry including many designer items; sterling items including Mexican; plastics including Bakelite, Lucite, and other plastics; accessory items including compacts, Florenza accessories, and purses. I have an inventory of thousands of items, but not everything is on the site. Feel free to contact me via e-mail about any requests.

Specialty: Hobé sterling items

Seeking: Designer jewelry

Contact: louise.champion@comcast.net

Organizations: VFCJ, JC, JR

No appraisals.

Comments: This site is the home to the California VFCJ auction which is held in the even years in conjunction with a VFCJ Mini Convention. We raise money for the VFCJ color fund. Though members can continue to bid at the convention, most items are won by online bidders. This year 75% of the winners were online bidders. You do not need to be a member to bid or to donate items, but you do need to be a member to attend the conventions. I maintain space in an antique mall on the San Francisco peninsula. It is called Antiques Then and Now, and is located on Industrial Ave. at the intersection of Britton and Industrial. I also do The Art Deco show which is held in San Francisco twice a year at the Concourse at 8th and Brannon. And I do the Hillsborough Antique show which is held at the San Mateo County Fair Grounds three times a year.

Amazing Adornments
Carolyn Henry
www.amazingadornments.com
Est. 2004

Offering: Amazing Adornments carries vintage, antique, and contemporary costume jewelry as well as vintage accessories, collectible vintage jewelry, and gentleman's accessories. I also have a small vintage ad section that I hope to enlarge in the future.

Specialty: Costume jewelry from the 1940s to the 1980s

Seeking: I would like to enhance my plastic jewelry, mainly high-end Bakelite. I am also looking for signed Trifari or Coro jelly bellies and vintage purses.

Contact: carolyn@amazingadornments.com

Buyer's wish list available.

Organizations: VFCJ, JC, JR, Silver Forum, Vintage and Collectable Costume Jewelry Ring, and Discovering Juliana Jewelry

No appraisals.

Comments: I want my website to be a fun and easy shopping experience for my visitors. I strive to enhance my site and my products on a regular basis. I am in the process of developing a resource section that I hope will be useful to my buyers. I have been told by many of my customers that I provide exceptional customer service and I strive to do so. I began my website in 2004. I sold vintage and newer jewelry at online auctions prior to the decision to start a website of my own. I have always loved costume jewelry. I have a background in fashion retailing and computers so it seemed like a natural fit. I not only own the shop, I am the web mistress.

Lasting Values Vintage Jewelry
Irene Testa
www.lastingvalues.com
Est. 2004

Offering: High quality costume jewelry and silver jewelry

Specialize: Scandinavian jewelry

Contact: lastingvalues414@aol.com

Organizations: VFCJ and JC

Appraisals: Costume and silver jewelry

Comments: I travel overseas especially to Sweden several times a year in search of more treasures for my clients. If it is not unique and of lasting value you will not find it on my website. I offer unsurpassed customer service and a satisfied customer is my best advertisement.

Past Perfection Vintage Costume Jewelry
Cheryl Killmer
www.pastperfection.com
www.rubylane.com/shops/pastperfection
Est. 2000

Offering: I carry signed and unsigned costume jewelry primarily from the 1940s to 1960s with an emphasis in unusual and eclectic pieces and also glitz.

Specialty: DeLizza & Elster jewelry, also known as Juliana

Contact: mail@pastperfection.com

Organizations: VFCJ, JC, Discovering Juliana Jewelry

No appraisals.

Comments: I have a category on my website which spotlights many of my favorite D&E sets and parures to help identify it. I am also glad to help others discover the wonderful attributes of my favorite jewelry by being available to answer questions by e-mail.

Michelle's Vintage Jewelry
www.michellesvintagejewelry.com
Est. 2002

Offering: Vintage purses, hats, compacts, and cufflinks

Specialty: Czechoslovakian jewelry is my favorite!

Seeking: Czech pieces — the more ornate or bold, the better

Contact: michelle@michellesvintagejewelry.com

Organizations: Jewelry Talk

No appraisals.

Comments: I currently have an inventory of over 3,000 pieces. I like to think of vintage jewelry as a wearable art. There are so many styles, and periods to collect. To get maximum enjoyment out of your collection, get a nice large jewelry armoire, so all of your jewelry is easy to view and you can quickly select what you will wear for the day. A large glass curio or china cabinet works well. You can enjoy all of your pieces every day and easily find your pieces to wear. You can use velvet forms, too, inside of the cabinets — a real artistic display. I love fun, beautiful, high quality vintage jewelry.

Forgotten Romance Collectible Costume Jewelry and Accessories
Yelena & Mark Zhilo
www.forgotten-romance.com
Est. 1999

Offering: Vintage costume jewelry and accessories, and some vintage linens

Specialty: European designer jewelry

Seeking: European designer jewelry, couture and runway pieces, early Miriam Haskell, Schreiner

Contact: yelena@forgotten-romance.com or dreameryz@aol.com.

Organizations: VFCJ and JC

No appraisals.

Comments: At Forgotten Romance you can always find not only collectible jewelry, those coveted pieces, but jewelry you would love to wear. We have unique, gorgeous, and phenomenal (my daughter insists on me using this word) jewelry. For all tastes, for all ages. For women and men, for young and old, and in any price range — from just a few dollars to thousands. I'm sure you will love our selection and our service. We value our customers and most of our business is repeat business. We welcome inquiries and will be happy to assist you in anything we can.

Jennifer Lynn's Timeless Jewelry
Jennifer Lynn Edie
www.jltimelessjewelry.com
Est. 2004

Offering: A diverse collection of jewelry from the Victorian era up through the 1960s. There are many luxurious unsigned jewels, as well as marvelous vintage costume and sterling silver jewelry from distinguished designers, manufacturers, and artists.

Specialty: Our passion for vintage and antique jewelry is broad. We find the uniqueness of vintage jewelry appealing and select those pieces that are of exceptional quality. Our inventory is a reflection of this and you will find an extensive assortment from which to choose.

Seeking: Good quality vintage jewelry in excellent condition

Contact: info@jltimelessjewelry.com

No appraisals.

Comments: You may notice the occasional contemporary piece, but these are sold for a special local Tulsa organization that finds homes for retired racing Greyhounds. This wonderful organization is Halfway Home Greyhound Adoption. Our love of animals may be even more apparent when you explore the extensive selection of animal figural jewelry that touches the heart. There are spectacular birds of paradise, dogs, cats, sea creatures, and magnificent horses. Many of these 1930s – 1940s pins and brooches are vermeil, jeweled with sparkling rhinestones or beautifully colored with enamels. We take pride in providing excellent customer service and a vast selection of vintage and antique jewelry. It is important to us that customers are completely delighted with their jewelry buying experience.

Lady Frog's Vintage Jewelry
Al & Gayla Esch
www.ladyfrog-vintage-jewelry.com
www.rubylane.com/shops/ladyfrogjewelry
Est. 2004

Offering: Costume jewelry

Specialty: 1950s through the 1980s

Seeking: Art Deco and Victorian. We would love to add more Bakelite and plastics to our collection.

Contact: theladyfrog@centurytel.net

Buyer's wish list offered.

Organizations: JC, JR, Discovering Juliana Jewelry

No appraisals.

Comments: My daughters and I have collected jewelry for about 30 years, and I never thought of selling until the guest room started overflowing into another bedroom. My daughters played with the jewelry as children, and then as teens wore it to proms. Now they have children that enjoy the jewelry as well. We have really enjoyed selling jewelry on the Internet as well as at antique and collectible shows and flea markets. We attend all of the Palmer Wirf Exposition and Antique shows in Oregon and Washington. We attend the JCL Productions which are in Oregon and Washington. You will also find us at the small street fairs. We would be happy to have you come by and say hello.

The Glitter Box Vintage Collectible Designer Jewelry
Sheila Pamifloff
www.glitterbox.com
Est. 1996

Offering: Vintage American and European designer costume jewelry, mid-century modernist studio art jewelry, vintage Mexican sterling designer jewelry, vintage Scandinavian jewelry, Arts and Crafts jewelry

Specialty: Vintage Mexican jewelry, vintage American costume jewelry, mid-century modernist studio art jewelry

Seeking: 1930 – 1950 American and European designer signed jewelry

Contact: pamfiloff@glitterbox.com

Organizations: American Society of Jewelry Historians, VFCJ, JC

Appraisals offered.

Comments: Since the beginning, I have been dedicated to presenting high quality jewelry that has been well researched in a variety of fields.

Antiques by Evelyn
Evelyn L. Phillips
www.antiquesbyevelyn.com
Est. 1999

Offering: Vintage and contemporary costume jewelry and accessories

Specialty: Coro/Corocraft, Figurals

Seeking: D&E Juliana, L/N; dress-fur-shoe clips, clear brilliant brooch or bracelet demis

Organizations: VFCJ, JC, Discovering Juliana Jewelry

No appraisals.

Comments: I have been collecting vintage and contemporary costume jewelry and accessories for more than 30 years. I update frequently and firmly believe that quality does not have to be expensive. Pricing is well below retail, with fast page loads, personalized ordering, and a wide selection of affordable quality costume jewelry and accessories. Currently, all shipping on the Antiques by Evelyn is free and includes delivery confirmation in the U.S.

Capricious Crowns & Jewels
Dinah Hoyt Taylor
www.capriciouscrowns.com
Est. 1999

Offering: Vintage costume jewelry and artisan jewelry, collectibles and custom equine clothing and accessories

Specialty: Vintage signed and unsigned, artisan handcrafted crowns and jewelry

Seeking: Mexican sets and wooden horse brooches

Contact: info@capriciouscrowns.com

Buyer's wish list offered.

Organizations: Alliance of Worldwide Jewelry Artisans, JC, VFCJ, Genesee Valley Arts Council

No appraisals.

Comments: I work in sterling silver and copper. I specialize in cuffs, linked bracelets, and unusual necklaces, crowns and tiaras. Custom orders accepted.

Remember When Vintage
Rita Perloff
www.rememberwhenvintage.com
Est. 2006

Offering: Vintage jewelry and beads

Specialty: Vintage sterling, cameos, and beads

Seeking: Always interested in better costume jewelry

Contact: rewhen@tias.com

Buyer's wish list offered.

Organizations: JC, Silver Forum, JR

No appraisals.

Comments: I shop carefully so I can offer buyers quality vintage jewelry at affordable prices. Satisfaction is guaranteed when you shop at Remember When.

Broadwater Rose Jewels
Nancy Galvin
www.broadwaterrosejewels.com
Est. 2001

Offering: Vintage collectible costume jewelry. Enjoy a memorable visit through our vintage inventory complete with Victorian and Art Deco jewelry, sparkling signed and unsigned rhinestone jewels, pearls, vintage copper and sterling jewelry, ladies' vintage accessories (hat pins, hand bags, compacts), and more!

Specialty: Wide assortment of signed, unsigned 1940s – 1950s rhinestone jewelry, Art Deco, vintage sterling (Napier and Monet), Mexican sterling, Majorica pearls, vintage copper (Renoir and Matisse), Regency, Weiss, scarab and mustard seed jewelry.

Seeking: Art Deco, vintage sterling (Napier and Monet), Mexican sterling, vintage copper (Renoir and Matisse), Regency, Weiss, scarab and mustard seed jewelry

Contact: vintagejewels@verizon.net, nancy@broadwaterrosejewels.com, myvintagejewels@hotmail.com

Organizations: Jewelry Central, Collectic Web Directory, Digital Women.com, JC, VFCJ

Appraisals: We offer our customers written assessments for personal vintage and collectible costume jewelry items (excluding fine jewelry items at this time). We assess and research information regarding vintage costume jewelry pieces and provide a written evaluation including the current market value based on our extensive experience. We provide the history and value of vintage jewelry item(s) for a small fee. We also encourage customers to visit the Jewelry Marks & Identification pages available at our website free of charge and provide book recommendations for additional research.

Comments: We have been in the antique business for over 10 years, and previously owned Weirwood Station Antiques. Now our comprehensive vintage jewelry collection is offered online and is available to purchase in person at Blue Crow Antique Mall located in Keller, Virginia, on the lovely Eastern Shore of Virginia. Broadwater Rose Jewels is also associated with Broadwater Antiques with wonderful gifts for *him* including vintage cuff links, fishing lures and reels, and smoking accessories!

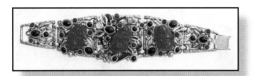

Forever Vogue Vintage Jewelry & Artwork
Annette Forslund
www.forevervoguevintagejewelry.com
Est. 2004

Offering: Vintage costume jewelry and accessories — artwork as well

Specialty: Unique, unusual, glitzy, well-designed pieces — signed as well as unsigned

Seeking: I am always looking for well designed pieces unmarked, as well as signature pieces by Haskell, Schiaparelli, Trifari, Boucher, Reja, Har, as well as European, Czech, Austria, Germany

Contact: Telephone: (630) 802-1211 or by e-mail: Ampsal91@aol.com.

Organizations: JC & VFCJ

No appraisals.

Comments: I love finding well-designed vintage costume jewelry. It's the design elements that I look for, the way it's constructed, signed or unsigned, it doesn't matter so much as the design quality, and construction, to me, that is most important. That's when you know you have a phenomenal jewelry piece! I want you to be satisfied when you receive your purchase and I want you to feel confident in buying from me in the future, so I'm meticulous with what I put on my website.

Vintage Costume Jewelry Dot Com
Jo-Ann Sturko
www.vintagecostumejewelry.com
Est. 2004

Offering: Glamorous jewelry from around the world, designer signed jewelry, sterling silver, handmade artisan jewelry, and a selection of fine estate jewelry

Specialty: Fashionable vintage pieces that complement modern fashion. Our inventory reflects a passion for unique glass beaded necklaces and dramatic earrings.

Seeking: We are always seeking interesting beaded necklaces, big earrings, Kenneth Jay Lane, French and Czech jewelry.

Contact: postmaster@vintagecostumejewelry.com

Organizations: JC

Appraisals: Due to the volume of requests we receive for information regarding jewelry, we have set up a service for people wanting to know about their items. More information can be found in the FAQ section of our site.

Comments: We sell items that best reflect the personalities of ourselves and our customers; sometimes quirky, often fun, and always classy. You will also find various well researched resource pages on topics dealing with vintage jewelry. Our descriptions are accurate and our pictures clear. If you are passionate about jewelry, you will want to stop by and take a look. We look forward to seeing you there!

Annie Sherman Vintage Jewelry
Annie Sherman
www.anniesherman.com
Est. 2003

Offering: Vintage costume jewelry

Specialty: Beautiful crystal rhinestone jewelry mostly from the 50s and 60s era.

Seeking: Anything vintage and beautiful!

Contact: annie96745@yahoo.com

Buyer's wish list offered.

No appraisals.

Comments: Please see my "Vintage Jewelry And Me" page at: www.AnnieSherman.com/me.html Also, my happy customers' comments at: www.AnnieSherman.com/praises.html

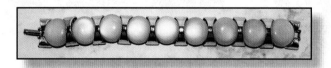

Eternal Jewels
Sheila Winters
www.eternaljewels.com
Est. 1988

Offering: Vintage costume and collectible jewelry. Victorian and silver jewelry. Bakelite jewelry.

Specialty: I have a preference for the unusual and funky. Designers are great but some of my favorite pieces are little "no names". Basically, I include jewelry in my website that I think people will enjoy "eternally".

Contact: sheilajwinters@eternaljewels.com

No appraisals.

Comments: I have a brick and mortar shop in McIntosh, Florida called Winters Past. We've been in business nearly 10 years and have a huge stock of vintage jewelry, hats, vintage clothing, etc...a very nice boutique! My website can only hold a very small portion of my inventory and I am always glad when customers stop by. We're at Avenue E and Highway 441 in McIntosh, FL. (352) 591-1455

Here are a few additional sites you may like to visit.

Sande Katttau at KATTSLAIR
www.rubylane.com/shops/kattslair

Claudia Roach at The Pink Lady
www.rubylane.com/shops/thepinklady

Lisa B. Boydstun at Gingerbread Farm Antiques and Vintage Jewelry
www.rubylane.com/shops/gingerbreadfarm

Kaye Aaroe Barbieri at KayeJaye Jewelry
www.rubylane.com/shops/kayejaye

Mariann Katz at Mariann Katz Original Designs and Vintage Costume Jewelry
www.ladywoodlane.com

Cindy Amirkhan at A TWINKLE in TIME Vintage Jewelry & Accessories
www.rubylane.com/shops/atwinkleintime

Linn Alber at Linn's Collection At Rainbows' End
www.rubylane.com/shops/linnscollectionatrainbowsend

Lorna Breshears at Jewelry Addiction
www.rubylane.com/shops/jewelryaddiction

Jeri Steenwerth at Jeri'z Joolz
www.rubylane.com/shops/jerizjoolz

Visit TIAS found at www.tias.com:

Kathleen Finderson at Glitter Gals
www.tias.com/stores/glittergals/

TACE
Terri Friedmanat
www.tace.com/vendors/rhumba.html

Lucinda Petersen at Elf 'n' Antiques & Collectibles
www.elfnantiques.com

VFCJ	JC	JR
Vintage Fashion & Costume Jewelry	Jewelcollect online jewelry club	Jewelry Ring Yahoo Group
Lucille Tempeta	www.lizjewel.com	Go to Groups on Yahoo for
vfcj@aol.com		information on joining

For additional information about VFCJ and JC please see my first book.

Bibliography

Baker, Lillian. *Fifty Years of Collectible Fashion Jewelry*. Paducah, KY: Collector Books, 1986.

Ball, Joanne Dubbs and Dorothy Hehl Torem. *Costume Jewelers, The Golden Age of Design*; Atglen, PA: Schiffer Publishing, 1990.

Ball, Joanne Dubbs and Dorothy Hehl Torem. *Masterpieces of Costume Jewelry*. Atglen, PA: Schiffer Publishing, 1996.

Cera, Deanna Farnetti. *Amazing Gems*. New York, NY: Harry Abrahms Inc., 1995.

Dolan, Maryanne. *Collecting Rhinestone and Colored Jewelry 4th Edition*. Books Americana, 1998.

Gordon, Angie. *Twentieth Century Costume Jewelry*. Adasia International, 1990.

Miller, Harrice Simons. *Costume Jewelry Identification and Price Guide, 2nd Edition*. Avon Books, 1994.

Moro, Ginger H. *European Designer Jewelry*. Atglen, PA: Schiffer, 1995.

Parry, Karima. *Bakelite Bangles Price & Identification Guide*. Iola, WI: Krause Publications, 1999.

———. *Bakelite Pins*. Atglen, PA: Schiffer Publishing, 2001.

Pullée, Caroline. *20th Century Jewelry*. Emmaus, PA: JG Press, 1997.

Rezazadeh, Fred. *Costume Jewelry, A Practical Handbook & Value Guide*. Paducah, KY: Collector Books, 1998.

Simonds, Cherri. *Collectible Costume Jewelry Identification & Values*. Paducah, KY: Collector Books, 1997.

Time-Life. *The Encyclopedia of Collectibles, Inkwells to Lace*. New York, NY: Time-Life Books, 1997.

Tolkien, Tracy and Henrietta Wilkinson. *A Collector's Guide to Costume Jewelry*. Richmond Hill, Ontario: Firefly Books, 1997.

Auction Catalogs:

Christie's East Couture Jewels: The Designs of Robert Goossens Wednesday 15 November 2000.

Index

Index